DENNIS POTTER

Dennis Potter's numerous television plays include *Blue Remembered Hills* (1979), *Brimstone and Treacle* (commissioned in 1975 but banned until 1987) and the series *Pennies from Heaven* (1978), *The Singing Detective* (1986), *Blackeyes* (1989) and *Lipstick on Your Collar* (1993). He also wrote novels, stage plays and screenplays. He died in June 1994.

DENNIS POTTER

Seeing the Blossom

Two Interviews,
a Lecture
and a Story

faber and faber
LONDON · BOSTON

First published in 1994
under the title *Seeing the Blossom:*
Two Interviews and a Lecture
by Faber and Faber Limited
3 Queen Square London WC1N 3AU
Reprinted twice; reissued 1994

Photoset in Linotype Ehrhardt by Parker Typesetting Service, Leicester
Printed in England by Clays Ltd, St Ives plc

Interview with Melvyn Bragg
© Channel Four Television Corporation, 1994
The James MacTaggart Memorial Lecture
© Whistling Gypsy Productions Ltd, 1993
Interview with Alan Yentob
© PFH (Overseas) Ltd, 1987
'Last Pearls' © PFH (Overseas) Ltd, 1994.
First printed in the *Daily Telegraph*, 4 June 1994.

Dennis Potter is hereby identified as author of this work in
accordance with Section 77 of the Copyright, Designs and
Patents Act 1988

A CIP record for this book is available from
the British Library

ISBN 0-571-17436-1

2 4 6 8 10 9 7 5 3 1

CONTENTS

To my dear Margaret . . .
Still the steadfast one.

Introduction

by MELVYN BRAGG

It is difficult to write about the interview I did recently with
Dennis Potter without feeling redundant. If anyone ever spoke
for himself, Dennis Potter did in that interview. I had an all but
overwhelming sense of apprehension then and it persists now.
Yet, by way of a foreword and to give these pieces the platform
they deserve, some notes on that last testament have been called
for, and may be in order.

Was it too opportunistic on my part to suggest the interview?
Michael Grade, Chief Executive of Channel 4, rang to tell me
that he had spoken to Dennis Potter and learned that he had
terminal and incurable cancer. He was kept going on painkilling
drugs, there were no more than a few weeks left.

Like everyone who knew Dennis Potter, well or slightly, I had
become used, almost hardened to that relentless illness –
psoriasis – which had made his body so painful since his mid-
twenties. His work and his voice were both so powerful and
fluent that they rolled over it and made it seem much less of an
affliction than it must have been. But this was different – cancer
of the pancreas and the liver.

Michael Grade, who knew him as I did, wanted to talk about
the man and the awful news and we talked, as you do, in terrible
regret for some time. Towards the end of our conversation he
reminded me of an interview I had done with Dennis and asked
if he could have it on stand-by. Of course. But, I said, it was
done in 1978. Would it be possible to ask Dennis if he would do
another interview? I was sure that he would not be offended at
the request. We would take no rights. If it did not work we would
scrap it. If it did, we would transmit it when he wanted it
transmitted. He could easily say no.

He said yes. He wanted to be interviewed in a television studio. It had to be early in the morning because that was when he had his fullest strength.

We set to work. It goes without saying that I have never prepared for an interview as thoroughly as I prepared for this, even though I knew his work well and had seen almost all of it as it had come out. But there were problems.

The central and most important problem was of course his health and stamina. His friend and agent Judy Daish who brought him to London the night before and, as it were, managed him throughout the whole business, had no idea how long he could sustain such an encounter. Twenty minutes? Forty? Her estimate did not go much further than that and she warned us that he could suddenly be taken so ill that we would have to cut it short or cut it altogether. Therefore every minute was precious. Therefore the line of questioning had to be simple, un-niggling and aimed to set him targets which he could go for. It also had to be capable of coming to an abrupt stop. My primary job was to enable him to say what he wanted to say. Nothing else mattered at all.

Those who worked on the programme with me at LWT were Christopher Walker who did research and Nigel Wattis and David Thomas, producers. Waldemar Januszczak at Channel 4 – the interview, should it work, was to be part of his *Without Walls* series – was also involved from the start.

There were other problems. They might seem trivial to readers but they were very important to us. Should we use stills or clips from the plays? Had this been a South Bank Show we would have taken it for granted that illustrations of the work were essential. But I thought that here they could somehow be intrusive. We decided against, even though we had reviewed the work and picked out excellent and illuminating passages. It proved to be the right decision, I think. It meant that for more than 95 per cent of the time we were concentrating on the face of the man facing his own life and death in a way which was to capture the emotions and the admiration of a considerable part of this nation. The simplicity and, if one can risk the word, the nakedness of it gave it luminous power.

How were we to begin? We decided to roll the camera from the moment we came into the studio. This would emphasize the television-work environment he wanted to be in. It would underline his loyalties and celebrate what he had always adhered to. In practical terms it would mean that we did not lose a second of what, for all we knew, might be rather a short interview. And again there was a simplicity and openness about it which fitted the event.

The main problem as far as I was concerned was to avoid mawkishness, sentimentality and any whisper of the wrong sort of intrusiveness. Or any sort of intrusiveness. The main purpose that I had was to give him as much space and time and energy as possible for as long as possible.

We met just after nine at the South Bank Studios. Despite very careful plans there was of course a bit of a cock-up as he and Judy Daish had wandered around for five or ten minutes. When I met him he was nervous and tetchy. I was having trouble with my own nerves. My job was to make him feel easy and clearly he was ill at ease. We met in a viewing room and had a drink of coffee but the atmosphere was not at that stage at all promising and, frankly, he looked very ill.

We had been told that his body heat fluctuated out of his control, and so the lighting man and the producers had been there since six in the morning putting in special filters and pulling all the lights as far back as they could to keep the place cool. We were told that he would not mind a drink, and champagne was a good kick-start. So there it was on the table beside him with the black coffee and the ashtray for his wonderfully defiant smoking. A flask of liquid morphine which he knew he would need he handed to me, so that I could give it to him quickly and unscrew the rather stiff top.

As we settled down we talked and both of us made that silent pact that can happen before an interview – the decision that we were going to go flat out for it. We kept in some of that short preamble and then, when everything was settled, made a formal beginning.

Obviously I could not put on an introduction before this particular interview. Given the nature of Dennis and myself it was impossible to tell him up front then how much I had enjoyed and been moved and annoyed and spurred on by so much of his work. The enchantment of *Blue Remembered Hills*, the magnificent cheek of *Pennies from Heaven*, the brilliance of *The Singing Detective*, the wrestling with Religion, the railing against an Establishment that was yet often seen affectionately . . . In several ways since he first came into print with *The Glittering Coffin* and on to the screen with *Nigel Barton* there have been elements of my own life and experience and imagined worlds in his work. As there have been, I am sure, for so many others, which is one of the reasons for the resonance that his writing has.

And I loved the way he had poured his talent with apparent recklessness into television. It was a medium which was and still is often thought of as merely ephemeral and just the people's forum. But it reaches out to a cross-section and range of people who can be contacted so directly in no other way. His is one of the talents which made television the true national theatre and the place where this country talked to itself. I rated the way that he took to television before the appearance of the video, with its consoling prospect of posterity.

What I suppose I hoped would hold the interview together was a shared sub-text. Our background experience had much in common – coal mining, grammar school, Oxford, journalism,

BBC television, London, and yet the inescapable pull of a beautiful part of England. Like all generations we often marched to the same drummer. Many others felt the same.

We settled down and began. I said that I would ask him about the cancer at the start. Yes, he said, let's get it over with. His answer to that first question flew like a bird on the wing. And on he went. Yes, I could have asked him other and more personal questions, but that's not the way I go and I hoped that, through the work, he would be released to talk about his deepest concerns. I think he did. Obviously more could have been done and it could have been different but within the eighty minutes, of which we trimmed about ten which were rather repetitious, we delivered – what?

We certainly delivered a television programme which moved and even rocked many of the people watching. Thousands of people reacted directly with phone calls and letters. For some it was a living example of great courage. For others it was an address to the nation in duplicitous and dangerous times. He spoke for sons and their fathers, England and its true traditions, for the present and its infections and yet its possibilities. Of his own work and his last remaining ambition, of the experience of being alive for now.

The response, as we all know, was quite extraordinary and unprecedented. There was a passion and a translucence before the fact of death and the dreadful pain which moved and impressed so many in a way that could have been achieved by no one else I can think of.

At the end he was all but exhausted. Frankly, all in the studio felt drained, and yet there was a feeling of relief and even exhilaration that the job had been done properly by him. After he had left, one of the cameramen came up to me and said, 'That was a privilege.'

After Dennis had gone – we had driven his car into the scene dock to make it easier – I went out on to the Embankment for a walk. It was raining quite hard. Somehow I was pleased about that even though I had no coat. The Thames – English as Potter is English – was running a high tide. London was about its massive and complex business. I found that I was clutching on deep breaths and, difficult to admit, holding back tears, hoping to God that what we had done had enabled him to say what he wanted to say. Hoping as well, as I walked towards St Paul's, for a miracle.

An interview with Melvyn Bragg,
Channel 4, April 1994

MELVYN BRAGG: *How did you, and when did you, find out that you'd got this cancer?*

DENNIS POTTER: Well, I knew for sure on St Valentine's day (*laughs*), like a little gift, a little kiss from somebody or something. Obviously I had suspicions . . . I had a lot of pain before then and there was a quite accidental sort of mis-diagnosis of the condition in London, here when I was on the wing on something, and an assumption being made that initially it was an ulcer or then a spastic colon, and all that sort of thing, which meant, unfortunately, because Margaret my wife was ill, and I was unwilling to leave her at that time, that I was not mixing up doctors. But in December and January in particular, I was trying to control, what in effect I now realize was the pain of cancer, with Panadol, which is ludicrous. In a way it was almost a relief to find out what it was, cancer of the pancreas with secondary cancers already in the liver and the knowledge that it can't be treated. There's no . . . neither chemotherapy nor surgery are appropriate, it's just simply analgesic care until, you know, Goodnight Vienna, as they say in football I believe nowadays. (*laughs*) . . . And I've been working since then flat out at strange hours 'cos I'm done in the evenings, because, mostly because of the morphine. The pain is very energy-sapping, but I do find that I can, I can be at my desk at five o'clock in the morning, and I'm keeping to a schedule of pages, and I will and do meet that schedule every day.

Obviously, I had to attend to my affairs as well. I remember reading that phrase when I was a kid, 'He had time to tend to his affairs' . . . But what it did give me also, yes, I always, I mean as a child, without question I know for a fact, and there's no argument about this, that I was coward. A physical coward. And often I'm also, I'm a very, I'm a really cripplingly shy person actually, I hate new situations, new people, with almost a dread. Now those two consequences in your adult life can really create serious wrong impressions of yourself to yourself, and of yourself to other people, because you try and compensate for what you know – (a) you're a coward, (b) you're shy – so that can lead to aggression and a sort of the obverse, the reverse of shy, the arrogance if you like, because you're wearing it like a cloak, in order to get through that particular . . . but to let *that* drop and find out that in fact at the last, thank God, you're not actually a coward. And I haven't shed a tear since I knew.

I grieve for my family and friends who know me closest obviously, and they're going through it in a sense more than I am. But I discover also what you always know to be true, but you never know it till you know it, if you follow (sorry, I've got . . . my voice is echoing in my head for some reason) . . . I think actually to you, I remember Martin Amis saying something about you reach your forties, your forties are middle age, and nobody ever tells you, nobody's ever told you, you know, what it's like. Well, it's the same about knowing about death. We all, we're the one animal that knows that we're going to die, and yet we carry on paying our mortgages, doing our jobs, moving about, behaving as though there's eternity in a sense. And we forget or tend to forget that life can only be defined in the present tense, it is *is*, and it is *now* only. I mean, as much as we would like to call back yesterday and indeed yearn to, and ache to sometimes, we can't, it's in us but we can't actually, it's not there in front of us. However predictable tomorrow is, and unfortunately for most people, most of the time, it's too predictable, they're locked into whatever situation they're locked into . . . Even so, no matter how predictable it is, there's the element of the unpredictable, of the you don't know. The only thing you know for sure is the present tense, and that nowness becomes so vivid to me that, almost in a perverse sort of way, I'm almost serene. You know, I can celebrate life.

Below my window in Ross, when I'm working in Ross, for example, there at this season, the blossom is out in full now ... it's a plum tree, it looks like apple blossom but it's white, and looking at it, instead of saying 'Oh that's nice blossom' ... last week looking at it through the window when I'm writing, I *see* it is the whitest, frothiest, blossomest blossom that there ever could be, and I can see it. Things are both more trivial than they ever were, and more important than they ever were, and the difference between the trivial and the important doesn't seem to matter. But the nowness of everything is absolutely wondrous, and if people could *see* that, you know. There's no way of telling you, you have to experience it, but the glory of it, if you like, the comfort of it, the reassurance ... not that I'm interested in reassuring people, bugger that. The fact is, if you see the present tense, boy do you see it! And boy can you celebrate it.

MB: *You said earlier that it wasn't to do with believing that life was eternal, but have you any feeling that, from the position you're in, it might be? You've said that you've never quite thrown off the idea of believing in God, and it features in a lot of your work ...*

DP: Well, yes, I don't know about ... Yeah, God's a rumour if you like, God is a ... I mean, the kind of Christianity, or indeed any other religion, that is a religion because of fear of death, or hope that there is something beyond death, does not interest me. I thought, what kind of cruel old bugger is God, if it's terror that is the ruling edifice, if you like, the structure of religion? And too often for too many people it is. Now that to me isn't religion.

Religion has always been – I've said it before, it doesn't matter that I repeat myself, I won't get many more chances to repeat myself, thank God – but religion to me has always been the wound, not the bandage. I don't see the point of not acknowledging the pain and the misery and the grief of the world, and if you say, 'Ah but God understands' or 'Through that you come to a greater appreciation' . . . I mean, I don't think, well you nasty old sod, if that's God . . . that's not God, that's not my God, that's not how I see God. I see God in us or with us, if I see at all, as some shreds and particles and rumours, some knowledge that we have, some feeling why we sing and dance and act, why we paint, why we love, why we make art. All the things that separate us from the purely animal in us are palpably there, and you can call them what you like, and you can theologize about them and you can build great structures of belief about them. The fact is they are there and I have no means of knowing whether that thereness in some sense doesn't cling to what I call me.

MB: *Do you spend much time thinking about your childhood and raking through that, Dennis, and the time in the Forest of Dean, the time with your parents?*

DP: I think any writer does. In particular writers, but I think everybody does. But I think in particular . . .

MB: *Because you've written about it often. Where is it now, as it were, in your . . .*

DP: Where is the Forest of Dean? It's still back there. It's a sort of mythic Forest of Dean. There's the real one (*laughs*), with the same signs and stresses as the real anywhere, and there's the other one . . . the one I grew up as a small child in, and those rather ugly villages in beautiful landscape. Just accidentally a heart-shaped place between two rivers, somehow slightly cut off from them, the rest of England and Wales on the far side, the other border, which is why as a border person I always hate the Welsh (*laughs*) . . . inevitably, you know, because I was brought up to. Yet many of my friends are Welsh! But the Relations Act cannot touch me here. I'm a border person and that's the way it is.

MB: *Do you look back and . . . I mean, a lot of people think that you see your childhood in . . . there are terrors in it, but it is some kind of place in England that was a particular period in the lives of a lot of people which was to do with a sense of community. Now, we've both been through that, and we know that things were wrong – awful and terrible and so on – but there's a glow there. Is it a glow because you're a middle-aged man looking back?*

DP: Well, it's partly that and it's partly . . . it's true the fact about childhood, which I tried to do in things like *Blue Remembered Hills*, for example. I used adult actors to play children in order to make them like a magnifying glass, to show what it's like. And because if you look at a child, talk about present tense, that's all they, all a small child lives in. So a wet Tuesday afternoon can actually be years long, and it – childhood – is full to the brim of fear, horror, excitement, joy, boredom, love, anxiety, every . . . you know, loss. Loss. I remember losing a pen once – the sleeplessness, the anxiety – I've lost my pen, oh my god, I've lost my pen . . . oh, the pen-ness of that pen, and the lostness of that loss is so great in child. Maybe you kind of revert to that in a way, but my Forest of Dean childhood, well . . . it is a strange and beautiful place, with a people who were as warm as anywhere else, but they seemed warmer to me, and the accent is almost so strong, it's almost like a dialect. (*Talks in this dialect, which is inaudible.*) Up the hill three times, well, twice actually, usually on a Sunday, sometimes three times to Salem Chapel and those little floppy, covered . . . orange-covered hymn books, Ira Sankey's *1,200 Sacred Songs and Solos* and all this . . . numbers would be slotted up on the board like those choruses, like . . . there's one I'm trying to – it's funny, I can think of the number before I can think of the chorus, I can see it as clear as though it were written in front of me on the slat – 787, hymn number 787: 'Will there be any stars, any stars in my crown, when the evening sun goes down, when I wake with the blessed in the mansion of rest, will there be any stars in my crown?' And, of course, it makes me laugh, and yet it tugs at me, and I see it. I see those little kids' faces singing 'Will there by any stars in my' – any stars, it's repeated – any stars, any stars in my crown?' and countless numbers of such things. And for me, of course, the language of the New Testament in particular, but the Bible in general was actually, as it is to a child. I don't know, I suppose even to a child brought up in Pinner or Wembley Park, it must be something similar, but it was the Holy Land – I knew Cannop Ponds by the pit where Dad worked, I knew that was where Jesus walked on the water; I knew where the Valley of the Shadow of Death was, that lane where the overhanging trees were. As I said, I was a coward. At dusk I'd whistle, going down that particular lane, but where I'm grateful for that language in a way, (a) that dialect, (b) that time in a sense where of course it's the war-time . . .

We were poor, yes. Dad was a coal-miner, reserved occupation, so he didn't go in the army. They've all closed now, those deep . . . the deep mine pits in the Forest of Dean – there were five of them when I was a child, deep shaft pits, and they were pick and shovel pits as well – bloody hard work; grinding shift work; grinding, grinding work. And there were, you know, no water closets . . . and the tin bath brought in in front of the coal fire and so on, on Friday night and all that, and men walking home with the coal dirt on them.

But the . . . the whole country at that time was politicized, even children knew what the war was about. I mean, we *did*, and the rumours (oh, there's a lot of rewriting of history – there always is, revisionist history always comes along). People say this and that, and they make . . . we British in general, English in particular – I find the word British harder and harder to use as time passes – we English tend to deride ourselves far too easily . . . because we've lost so much confidence, because we lost so much of our own sense of identity, which had been subsumed in this forced Imperial identity which I also obviously hate. But we were, at that time, both a brave and a steadfast people, and we shared an aim, a condition, a political aspiration if you like, which was shown immediately in the 1945 General Election, and then one of the great governments of British history – those five, six years of creating what is now being so brutally and wantonly and callously dismantled was actually a period to be proud of, and I'm proud of it.

You don't mind this cigarette? I just . . . now . . . I mean, I always have smoked, but . . .

MB: *Why should I mind?*

DP: Well, people do nowadays. You get so bloody nervous smoking.

MD: *It's all right, I'm a very passive smoker.*

DP: Thank God I don't have to go to America any more . . . because I remember asking a waiter in America at breakfast for an ashtray as he was turning away, and it was just as though I'd shot him in the back. It's easier to pull a gun in America than a cigarette out of your pocket. But I like to go in the . . . there is a remnant left on the train – I do, of course, travel first class; I mean, I enjoy money and spending it . . . money, I like it . . . but in the remnant of the first-class train, InterCity, there is one bit for smokers, and if I . . . I love to see . . . if I see people sitting there without a cigarette, I love to say, 'You do know this is a smoking compartment, don't you?' Because I've so many, you know . . . 'You do know you're not allowed to smoke here.' But of course now I'm just virtually chain-smoking, because there's no point in . . . There's so many things, like I can't keep food down any more – I can't have a meal, my digestive system's gone, but I can drink things, and those prepared, those horrible chemical things with all the minerals and stuff in them, but I can add a dash of this and that to it, which I do, and . . . like cream, like cholesterol, aawww! I can break any rule now, you know, I can do it ... but the cigarette, well, I love stroking this lovely tube of delight. Look at it (*laughter*).

MB: *I've packed in. Now stop, or I'll be smoking again in a minute, Dennis, with you. It, it's been written about so much and derided so much, people from working-class backgrounds getting to Oxford and doing what ...*

DP: Yeah.

MB: *... or university, but in your case Oxford, and yet it is, it is a ... that little journey is quite, is not an easy one to make, is it?*

DP: It's a long journey. It should be easy, but any journey from adolescence to adulthood is a long one.

MB: *What did it do to you, do you think, going from the Forest of Dean to ... It's a big jump, I know.*

DP: Well, I'd already made a jump in one sense to London. My mother was a Londoner, her mother was a Forest of Dean woman who, in the parlance of the time, went into service – that was ... you know, it was a skivvy and a drudge, a servant in a London house – and met a Fulham plumber and married him – had, my mother's mother, I mean, the usual eleven, twelve kids and all that, and my mother used to come down to the Forest of Dean to visit her mother's family with her mother, and one weekend she met this young ... my dad was a ... he was such a gentle man, my father – he died in 1975. I still have a very good ... I have a better relationship with him than I could manage, as it were, at the time of the later stages of my so-called journey from grammar school to Oxford and all that that meant, which sort of slightly intimidated him.

MB: *What do you mean by a better relationship?*

DP: A better relationship in the sense that I see more and I feel that I understand more of his gentleness and of his desire to reach me, and I feel that I am being reached ... I can't put it in any other way. For example, the things he used to ... he used to be almost scared of me, when I didn't want him to be, and I used to feel irritation about that, which I didn't want to feel. You know, those sort of things. And I'd be writing in this little downstairs room, 'cos I've always, I've always had this passion for it. I have this antique – and I'm not ashamed now of being able to say, it is an antique word, and it's one that's easily scoffed at – but I do have a sense of vocation, and I have it to the, I will have it to the last ounce of my life, the last second. I had the sense, and I'm proud that I've got it, and I'm no longer ashamed of saying yes, I have had, have had a sense of vocation, and it was writing. And he would sort of hover on, in the doorway, or lean against the door jamb and, 'So . . . so, all right, our Den?' I'm writing, so I'd be irritated because, I mean, I'd go in and talk to him, I was finishing something, or I was doing, or I was engaged in something. 'Yes, Dad, sure' – you know all that, so 'Sure, it's all right – mind?' That anxiety to communicate but doing it wrongly. Now of course I'd say, 'Come on in, Dad, for Christ's sake sit down and let . . .' it doesn't matter about that now, that minute, but of course I cut my cards, and yet there's a sense in which by even saying it you see I've done it, I've said it – 'Come on in, Dad' – and he, he and I, I can feel him genetically in me, and I see the waste of so much of his life because of the system that he lived through. He was shy, he was gentle, he was a bit feckless in many ways. If he had a . . . he'd always say, the pound in your pocket is your best friend, but of course as soon as he had one, it'd be drinks all round in the pub, much to my mother's dismay, but he was that kind of, you know, 'Come on, us gotta have one', that kind of man. And I . . . I plug into that now more, more easily, that's all I can say.

MB: *Do you think that you've had . . . your driving themes in your work have come from this part of your childhood or did they come from what happened after the break to university and the first few years' university journalism?*

DP: Dunno, Melvyn. They . . . they come as you grow, and your childhood remains. I mean, I forget, I've forgotten who said it, but I remember reading some essay by some writer saying that for any writer the first fourteen years of his or her life are the crucible anyway, no matter what you do. But of course you add on and you use your experiences and I, I've always deliberately, as a device, used the equivalent of a novelist's first-person narrative. You know when the novelist says I, he doesn't mean I, and yet you want him to mean I, and I've used, for example in *The Singing Detective*, I used the Forest of Dean, I used the physical circumstances of psoriatic arthropathy, which, you know, still, you know, I've still got bloody psoriasis itching away at me, which is a bugger – you'd think *that* would lay off now, wouldn't you, but it won't! But I used that, and geographical realities, and it seemed so personal then, but I often do that. It isn't. I make it up, the story. You know the wife thing? The whole inner structure of that man is different to me. Now he was a man, the 'Singing Detective', Michael Gambon character, the Philip Marlow in a hospital bed at the beginning who had nothing. He was stripped of everything. He had no faith in himself, no belief in any political, religious or social system. He was full of a witty despair and cynicism. Now I have never been like that, and the dramatic story was very simple. It was simply seeing a man pick up his bed and walk. It's interesting, I always fall back into biblical language, but that's, that again, you see, is part of my heritage, which I in a sense am grateful for.

MB: *Do you feel you were thought of at one stage as a political writer, at a very early stage? Your first appearance on television was talking about class to some . . .*

DP: Yes.

MB: *. . . in some documentary programme.*

DP: Yes, that's right.

MB: *And then* Stand Up, Nigel Barton, *you stood as a Labour candidate, you worked with the* Daily Herald *and so on. Where does that figure now, Dennis, and when did it figure? Was it a . . .*

DP: It was part . . . it was part of the, it's the sort of subversive, you know, like there's . . . In pain there's such a thing as referred pain . . .

MB: *Yeah.*

DP: . . . and so on. It was part of the process of finding what writing was about. It was the same thing really. To me at Oxford when I was . . . the only way I could sort of express it then, you know, via *Isis* and articles, and I wrote a piece for the *New Statesman* when I was an undergraduate, things like that, and I realized that somewhere along the line my pen was actually going to provide me with a living. Politics seemed the gateway. My very first book I wrote as an undergraduate, although a printing strike delayed it until a year after I left Oxford — it came out in 1960.

MB: The Glittering Coffin?

DP: . . . called *The Glittering Coffin*, yes, which was a kind of metaphor for the condition of England. Typical young man's title, you see, typical piece of that sort of humbugging, canting rhetoric, which young men — bless their hearts — specialize in. I think we should always look back on our own past with a sort of tender contempt. As long as the tenderness is there, but also please let some of the contempt be there, because we know what we are like, we know how we hustle and bustle and shove and push and . . . and you sometimes use grand words to cloak it — one does — I'm not looking at you specifically, so don't squirm (*laughter*).

MB: *Just associating bodily there.*

DP: Politics was . . . seemed the door, until I actually stood as a candidate. By then, of course, illness had descended and I had a walking stick and I, I was drowning actually, drowning, felt that I was . . . On the *Daily Herald* I hated every second of it. And that world of popular journalism, as I saw it then, and the *Herald* eventually mutated through the mismanagement of the Mirror Group, its eventual owners, into ... There's an interesting thing ... as an old plot ... as a writer you will know, one of the favourite fantasy plots of a writer is a character's told you've got three months to live and – which is what I was told – and you, *who would you kill?* (*laughs*), 'cos you've got every ... and I'd call my cancer, the main one, the pancreas one, I call it Rupert, so I can get close to it, because the man Murdoch is the one who, if I had the time – in fact I've got too much writing to do and I haven't got the energy – but I would shoot the bugger if I could. There is no one person more responsible for the pollution of what was already a fairly polluted press, and the pollution of the British press is an important part of the pollution of British political life, and it's an important part of the cynicism, and misperception of our own realities, that is destroying so much of our political discourse.

MB: *You do feel the state of decay has deeply set in, don't you?*

DP: I do. With great regret and pity and ... and a feeling of shame, of self-shame too, but it's rescuable, just. It's up to people to stand up and shout a bit. Not to turn it into cynicism, which is, I'm afraid, what is happening. Politics is still crucially important. Our choices are vital, and we've got to make them and not just say, 'Oh they're all the same, they're all ...' They are all the same in certain ways, alas – a political animal is such an animal – but the ideas behind it, the concepts lurking some-where behind their rhetoric and their spittle and so on are important choices that we should make.

MB: *Do you think the overall sense of decay that you've talked about stems from political decay or political decay stems from other powerful symptoms?*

DP: Both, both. They interlace, the press and politics. The commercialization of everything means, of course, you're putting a commercial value upon everything and you turn yourself from a citizen into a consumer. We're not citizens, we're consumers, and politics is a commodity to be sold, and that's what is happening. And look what's happening at the BBC. Look what's happening to television in general. Look who runs it. The arguments by respectable, liberal commentators, liberal – small 'I' – commentators about size; the economies of scale and so on. They're all actually nonsense. A programme costs what a programme costs to make. It can be made by a tiny company. What they're talking about is ownership of the *means* of communications. And they're talking about 'the mass media' as J. B. Priestley coined the phrase; they're talking about political control in the end; they're talking ... how can we have a mature democracy when newspapers and television, where there's standard television, cable television is beginning to be so interlaced in ownership terms? Where are our freedoms to be guaranteed? Who is going to guarantee them? Look at the power that Murdoch has. Look at the ... the effects of all these take-overs and, you know, it's *not about programmes*. Now, the world that you and I came into, television or radio, when we came into it, I'm not saying that world wasn't paternalistic, and I'm not saying it can be preserved as it was, and I'm not saying there musn't be change, but that world was based upon a set of assumptions that are almost now derisible, laughable. Like in politics, certain statements become derisible. We're destroying ourselves by not making those statements. Just as we're destroying our television. Week by week, day by day, I see it.

If I were starting out now ... my first television programme was in 1960, a documentary about the Forest of Dean, my first television plays were in 1965, when I had this burst of energy ... through illness, when I reinvented myself, quite consciously, as an act. I was so out of it – I obviously had lost my job, I had two small kids and a third on the way, and I wrote this television play and they liked it, thank God, and commissioned another, and I had the ... I was given the space to grow into, and I gave, I gave my working life to it as a result, and I have, I have stayed with television to such a large extent because of that. Whereas if I was starting now, where would I get that chance? Who would cosset and look after me? Where is the single play? And the series, you can punch the buttons in the predictability ... You can call the shot numbers out in advance. The formula-ridden television is because of sales, because ... the nerve is they'll soon have, where they'll tell every five seconds who's switching off. The pressure upon creators, whether they're writers, directors, designers, actors, producers, whatever, that pressure will be all the time until you maximize your audience at any given point, which is the very antithesis of discovering something you didn't know. It's the very antithesis of the kind of broadcasting on television which was such a glory in British life.

MB: *But given what was done in the sixties and seventies on television, and given the power and influence of television, and given the fact that people came through from good schools and burgeoning universities – let's be a bit Panglossian about that – but given that, why do you think it turned so sharply in the mid-eighties and the country was and people were available to be turned round, and in a sense turned over?*

DP: Because there needed, there needed to be some stripping out of things, there needed to be change. We were conscious of the need for change and for a change in British politics, like the '45 government in a way. There was a genuine radicalism in the air – it was coming from the right. But then it became that everything was given, in a sense, its price tag, and the price tag became the only gospel and that gospel in the end is a very thin gruel indeed, and if you start measuring humankind in those terms, everything else then becomes secondary, or less important, or in some sense, as I say, laughable, and all the things that bind us as a community, whether it's ... they're partly right-wing things, you know. Sometimes I get out of bed and I don't know whether I'm right-wing or left-wing to be honest, 'cos I feel the pull of both. I feel the pull of tradition, and I love my land. I love England, and when I'm abroad, when I'm ... that's one of the things I don't have to do that any more, but I genuinely feel homesick. I don't mean ... I mean for an idea, almost, and I've always loved my country, but not at the expense, not flags and drums and trumpets and billowing Union Jacks and busby soldiers and the monarchy and the pomp and circumstance and all that, but the real – something about our people that I come from and therefore respond to, and I expect other people to do it of their own backgrounds and nations and cultures too.

But those things are very difficult to put prices upon and to quantify in the terms, terminology, of Mrs Thatcher and her successors. The current government will use phrases like community care when they mean, close that costly thing and put that madman on to the street. And then if it's in front of their noses, they'll do another temporary makeshift measure and claim that things are getting better, or that the spending has gone up. So what? It may have done, but what has actually happened, what is actually happening when a young person in many, many, many a town in this country sees no prospect of a job ... and then they say, they will moralize, that's the worst thing, and say, 'Oh crime is everything to do with the criminal.' What is the life of not expecting to get work? What is the life of only expecting cynicism in political conversation? What is the life that sees no horizon further than the latest nasty video and the cable TV and the Murdochs and the *Sun*? Just pick up a copy of the *Sun* and say, 'Is this Britain? Is this what we've done to ourselves?' Are these people, the people who work on that paper, how can they go home and face their families without any sense of shame? You know, I'd be ashamed to the pit of my guts if I were forced to do, and some of them are, to be fair, forced to do it because they don't want to be unemployed. They want to earn. They need to earn. Some of them do things that they are appalled by. I know that, I've met some of them. I know they are, but my God, what a system.

MB: *In your own writing ... There was a time when it seemed to me, and to a lot of people, that there were novels being written and plays being put on on stage and films being made, but the power of very good writers, directors, cameramen talking to a large public was on television and you were pushing it again and again. You were bringing up ideas of the devil, you were bringing up ideas of dialogue turning into singing. You were bringing up ideas of memory matching with fantasy and so on. Did you ... you obviously found television available to everything you wanted to do, and you made it available for a lot of other people.*

DP: It could be and can be and I, I reached a stage and I've written so many things down over so many years of working for television – obviously, I'm fifty-eight. I might reach my ... fifty-nine on 17 May. I might get there. It'd look neater, wouldn't it, to die fifty-nine? But technique, I don't think about any more. It's just natural to me, I don't even ... it's like with a musician ...

MB: *What about subject matter? Was there anything ... did you feel that you were being daring doing any of the things you did in it? Did you think, I am going to be ...*

DP: That's the only thing I really resent, that's the only thing I would stamp my foot about. I never have ... this is, I was going to say the gospel truth, here I go again, but this is the *truth*, Melvyn, that I have never felt the need to do that. It has come, the mould, if broken on any one point, has come out of the need to do what I was doing. Not, 'How do I break the mould?' It's the other way round, so things have happened. The way they come, I remember, it's ... it always sounds so mundane but, for example, the use of adults to play children in *Blue Remembered*

Hills was, is just, I was starting to write about children and I wanted to write something difficult because children don't have long speeches, you can't have flashbacks to non-existent memories. You can't have certain rhetorical devices. You have to have a continual twitchy action because that's how children move. And these were a group of seven seven-year-olds, and the only, ultimately the only, way I could see, while keeping exactly to the language of childhood and the movements of childhood and the constant present tense preoccupations of childhood, to show it without that filter coming in the way, which an audience going 'Ah, children' and immediately pushing it back to childhood, was by using *adults*, seven adult actors. Once you get over the panic of the first five minutes, when I think, my God, is this . . .? Colin Welland's great fat arse and great shorts addling, sploshing through mud making aeroplane noises, and chewing on an apple, and I thought, oh, you know, it's like one of those, it's going to be one of those dire, dread embarrassments, because it ain't gonna work. And yet people could see that it was . . . after a while people could see obviously that these were adults. Obviously, I mean, that goes without saying, but they also saw that they were children, so it worked. It wasn't because I was trying – do you see what I'm getting at? I was trying to show childhood not at one remove but straight on.

MB: *What about bringing in popular songs, as you did, say, with* Pennies from Heaven?

DP: That, I wanted to write about – in a sense it sounds condescending, and I don't mean it quite this way – I wanted to write about the way popular culture is an inheritor of something else. You know that cheap songs so-called actually do have something of the Psalms of David about them. They do say the world is other than it is. They do illuminate . . . this is why people say, 'Listen, they're playing our song', or whatever. It's not because that particular song actually expressed the depth of the feelings that they felt when they met each other and heard it. It is that somehow it re-evokes and pours out of them yet again, but with a different coating of irony and self-knowledge. Those feelings come bubbling back. So I wanted to write about popular songs in a direct way, it became just a technical problem for me. I thought, oh my. Not interested in writing a musical. A musical has a different grammar ... the action builds to a song and then a song caps it and then it moves on and the song is, you know, has a different function in a musical. It was, how do I get that music from way down there in the bag, or here in the ear, or at the side, how do I get it straight bang up front? And then I thought, well, they lip-synch things now and again. You know, like sometimes there's a bad performance or they dub from one language to another that way. Why don't I just try making the actor move his lips to the words of the song and see if it ... Then I tried it a bit, I tried it with myself in a mirror, and that was fun. I mean, I was a great singing pad, pre-karaoke, and, ah, again you see, rather than looking, I wasn't breaking a mould as such. I just found the ideal way of making these songs so real.

MB: *Dislike, and I can understand it, the use of this word controversial, but there were many times, but let's take a couple of times, when you really seemed to bump into opinion in this country. Your ... on this most popular extraordinary medium of television, which is doing things in the sixties and seventies in this country, and in many areas which people had never dreamt it could do, in terms of original writing in your case, it was reaching out in all directions, let's leave it at that, and taking on the public in a big way, there were ... Let's, can we talk about two times you really sort of bumped into them. One is to do with the, when you brought the notion of the de... we'll talk* Brimstone and Treacle, *the vision of a devil, the other was to do with sex in* Blackeyes. *Now sometimes these two things are directly related, but let's talk about them one at a time. What do you think*

20

was happening in the Brimstone and Treacle *row and then in the, in the business of sex on television?*

DP: Ah, *Brimstone and Treacle* was ... Can I break off for a second? I need a swig of that, there's liquid morphine in that thing. I'll keep going but I ... Can you unscrew that cap? I ... this is not agitation about *Brimstone and Treacle* by the way.

MB: *Do you want another drink?*

DP: I wouldn't mind, yes. (*Gets up, then returns.*)

MELVYN BRAGG: *Are you feeling OK? How much ... how much time?*

DENNIS POTTER: It's better to go on.

MB: *Right. Why do you think you got so much resistance in* Brimstone and Treacle?

DP: It's a very complicated story, but if I could put in essence what I saw I was trying to do – it's, in a way it's a simple flip-over of an orthodox, of an ordinary sentimental religiose, rather than religious, parable, in that there is an afflicted house – variously afflicted, but in particular with a crippled, seemingly mindless, struck girl, young girl. And there is a visitor, and the visitor brings her to life and makes her speak. Now, if that visitor were an angel, then all you would have is sanctimoniousness, you would learn nothing about anything, and I chose, in my head – and this is how it began, this is why I'm talking this way – it began in my head as like that ... What if it were the devil? Instead of making that easy distinction which, on the whole, only the blasphemous make ... non-religious people make this distinction very easily, between so-called good and so-called evil, when of course they are interrelated, and one is defined in terms of the other, and one can't exist without the other, which is why ... satan was an angel, you know ... and all art of any kind has attempted to deal with this, has had to deal with the dualism of it. So instead of the angel coming and rescuing the cripple and the dumb and the afflicted, I had the devil do it. The evil act can lead to good consequences; a good act can lead to evil consequences. This is often the case, and it is . . . it is incomprehensible. It is as though, you know, the rain falls on the just and upon the unjust. *It is so.* Now, it appeared disgusting because it was a devil, and because it was a rape, or the beginnings of a rape, that made her cry out; and interestingly, the cry out was actually an accusation against her father. That complexity is, as I say, simply a reversal of what would have been sanctimonious and sentimental. It was that that offended and afflicted people.

I remember Alastair Milne, Director of Programmes for television at the time, saying, in a letter to me, something like, 'brilliantly made and written, so and so . . . but nauseating' – 'nauseating, diabolical', exactly the right word. It *was* diabolical. It was meant to be. Nauseating, not in the sense that he meant, but nauseating in the sense of making you think about those forces, those circumstances, those afflictions, and the way we manipulate the words good and bad. That to me is what it was about.

MB: *It did, it did . . . it's strange that that should be banned, isn't it, in a way? Did you want to pursue it?*

DP: Now, Mrs Whitehouse wanted me prosecuted for blasphemy after *Son of Man* about Jesus, because my Jesus was, if you like, a Forest of Dean Jesus, with a view of the wood and the cross before his crucifixion, like knowing that it was good timber, and then the uses that man, cruel man, puts timber . . . instead of making tables and chairs and useful things, they kill other men with it – and because he was that sort of Jesus, and there are millions of Jesuses – obviously, and mine was just one of them – but there was a row in the Australian Parliament about it, you know, things like that, and I think, well, if people get so conditioned that they'll watch these endless pappy series without any . . . there's violence every twenty or thirty seconds – whatever the audience rating system demands – there's sex used just like that, bang . . . there are constant sanctimonious references to God or the good, you know . . . If you quest, if you try and make people see the real, real, real use of these words, they get hopping mad sometimes, but so be it. But that's what television's for too.

MB: *What about the outrage about sex in, say,* Blackeyes, *for instance?*

DP: Well, a lot of that . . .

MB: *What was going on there?*

DP: . . . was invited. It was a piece about alienation and it was alienating, and . . . and I did alienate, and I wanted to and I went too far. I wanted to show a lot of things going on at the same time. What I specifically wanted was to show what the Marxists would call reification of all that . . . the way that people are turned into things, and the way what is both the oldest and in some sense in the political language the newest ruling class, men; the way they have so consistently used women in . . . advertising, in fiction, in drama . . . in real life, most importantly of all, as . . . sexual commod... as things, you know, and there is a line in *Blackeyes*, said by Jessica, in which she says, 'There's no way that you, nor any other man, could ever understand what it is that you men make us women think of our bodies.'

Now, the trouble is, it's written by a man – me. That was my dilemma. So I, I did several things at the same time: I made an ironic narrative with, as though it were me, myself as a character, in *Blackeyes*, which was saying, 'Yes, yes, I'm being seduced, I am seducing you, I am showing you . . .', instead of, like, the old *News of the World* exposing a brothel, 'I then made my excuses and left', you know, I stayed and screwed, as it were, because I wanted to show it. But of course it's like a pack of hounds; you know what happens – once it starts, they . . . once it starts, they won't see, they refuse to see, they can't see, and I was suddenly television's Mr Filth, I think the *News of the World* called me.

Dirty Den in the *Sun*. I felt personally soiled by it actually. On the whole, I'm, I'm, I have been blessed with a temperament that doesn't actually get very agitated about critics. I just think, up you, you know. So, I'm lucky that way, but this one, this particular lot, really got to me, because the ... the accusation by quite intelligent people that I was a misogynist really hurt me, because I know I'm not, and some of the ... You see, the trouble is that all political and ideological movements have labels and party lines, which some people just spill out when necessary.

The very intelligent feminists, the Kathy Ackers of this world, although I don't know whether feminism would now call Germaine Greer a feminist or not. I admire her, because she visibly changes her mind about things, and writes from her own experience ... I've never met her ... writes from her own physical and emotional experiences about what she really feels, and therefore what she thinks about the world, and she could see, I mean, she said something very rude – I think it was on television that I saw it – you know, that he might be an uptight little shit, but he's actually telling the truth. So I was relieved that people like that could see, but I was amazed by a number of intelligent women ... Now, for example, what would have happened if that had been *Blackeyes* by Denise Potter?

MB: *When you knew you were ... you had cancer, you decided to write. One of the things you decided to do was write. What are you writing? We're about a month on from when you were told, from 14 February.*

DP: Yes, I've done a lot. Yes. First of all I was on the point of delivery of something that had been commissioned quite a long time ago, called *Karaoke*, for the BBC. That *Karaoke* ... although there's a little bit set in the karaoke clubs, obviously karaoke is a metaphor ... there's the music, and you have your little line, you can sing it, and everything is written for you, and that is the way life appears to a lot of people and feels to a lot of people. For some you haven't got much space, and even the space you've got, although you use your own voice, the words are also written for you. So I'm using that as the metaphor, and I was on the point of delivering it, then this terrible . . . as soon as the news, as soon as I knew I was gonna die, I thought, I can't deliver this, this . . . whatever I'm doing now is my last work, and I want to be proud . . . I want it to be, I want it to be fitting, I want it to be a memorial. I want to speak, I want to continue to speak, and at the same time, you see, I have this, to me, a very exciting idea – I mean, I would say that, but I do feel the excitement of it, with Channel 4, which I'm calling *Cold Lazarus*, and you'll see why. You see, I'm trying to join two things that are currently in the air together. One is virtual reality, where you put on goggles and a pair of gloves, and you can actually – well, obviously, you land a plane simulated or you can, you can begin to have, they hope, and this is the commercial money behind it, you can almost feel that you're having sex with Marilyn Monroe or somebody, you know what I mean? But the computer world, virtual reality, it will invade (a) the entertainment business, but also (b) your own senses of reality . . . and you can use it in work, you know, and architecture, in whatever . . . that it is very, very, very much a thing of the future that is going to influence a lot of the ways we think about what we know about ourselves. And the other, using cryogenics – that is deep-freeze, that is the technology at absolute zero temperature – where, of course, it would be in California, where every nut roll will sooner or later end, they are actually freezing bodies of people, very rich people on the point . . . and there are some corporations making quite a lot of nice money out of this, freezing very rich people for eventual regeneration when they can cure whatever it is they died of. Now, one of . . . now they've honed that down, I discover they only need to freeze the head, so they can . . . you just have the head, and they will regenerate with hope. They've managed apparently to regenerate some frozen rat brain cells, which is interesting, but I have this series, you see, where there's the head, in its case, and all the electrodes are attached to it, and as they gradually thaw and stimulate the billions upon billions of brain cells, they discover that he's alive and there is memory there somewhere, real memory, and we're now talking about 400 years from now, and that real memory is of the thirties, forties, fifties, sixties – in other words, my memories, or what I choose to make my memories, and in order to stimulate those memories, they have to use virtual reality memories as well. Now, a high mogul type, the entertainment business, God knows what it would be like then, but a Murdoch successor, you know, when you can imagine entertainment really is the function of the world – wall-to-wall everything, helmeted or people won't know what's real and what isn't – looking at the monitors that are plugged into these real memories of those distant days of 400 years ago and the strange world in which people could walk safely in the streets and things like that, suddenly realizes he's on to an absolute winner. They plug this into the nightly entertainment, these real memories, and of course the man by then knows, although he's just a head, that . . . and wants the truth that we need to be mortal, we need to die, and he wants to, but now he's part of the entertainment business and his real memories mixed up with, not a satire, but mixed up with the world as though it's sort of the *Brave New World* or *1984* or whatever, but the same impulse that made those do it is joining virtual reality and cryotechnology, cryogenics together. Now, what I want to do, and this is . . . I'm floating this now publicly, so I'm gonna compromise some people, is the one . . . *Karaoke* – I've got a dry mouth . . . it's excitement . . . excuse me – *Karaoke* is the BBC, *Cold Lazarus* is at Channel 4. I want the man whose head is in the box and wired up and spilling out memories of the real world that I know to be the man who is the central character of

Karaoke. So what I would like – I don't have to break the thread I'm working on, I've got something, I just – all I hope is that I've got enough days to finish it, and I'm working all the hours I can and I'm making about . . .

I've got a GP in Ross, Paul Downey, whose name should be celebrated if I do finish this, who has so gently and carefully led me to a balance between pain control and mental control where I can work, that he's allowed . . . he's given me the liberty and he's had the intelligence to see that I can create a space to do ten pages a day, flat out, which is what I . . . when I go flat out I go flat out, and believe me, with a passion I've never felt, I feel I can write anything at the moment. I feel I can fly with it, I feel I, I can really communicate what I'm about and what the world . . . and what I feel, and what the world ought to know. I have a . . . that's all right . . . vocation, I've a passion about it, a conviction about it. What I'd like to see, since it is my last work, and since I have spent my life in television, and since that life has not been insignificant in television, I would like the BBC's part to be shown first by the BBC and repeated the same week on Channel 4, and then that inherited audience for the second part, *Cold Lazarus*, which would have some continuity in terms of character, but could still be . . . stand separately, obviously, to be shown first by Channel 4 and repeated by BBC.

Now, there are two men in whom I place some hope, in particular in the administrative . . . ways, I mean, in British television, whom I place a great deal of hope in, and in a way I'd like their roles reversed. One of them is Michael Grade, of whom I've always been very, very fond, as it happens, and the other is Alan Yentob. Now, if I've got . . . I haven't got space for meetings and things, and this programme is like, is my day for this, you know, right? If I could get those two together . . . Alan Yentob, in my opinion, should run Channel 4, and there is no question in my mind Michael Grade should be the Director-General of the BBC. That's what it's crying out for. Anybody with any nous can see that. But whichever, whatever, if Alan Yentob and Michael Grade would sit down with me and if I've got the half-hour away from my page, and if I've got the time to finish and, and – I almost said pray God then, but I don't mean it in that sense, I mean if . . . my only regret is is to die four pages too soon – if I can finish, then I'm quite happy to go. I, I don't mind, you know. I am quite serene. I'm not . . . I haven't had a single moment of terror since they told me. I know I'm going to die, whether it's in four weeks' time, five weeks' time, six weeks' time, it might be longer. I might make eight, nine, ten, who knows? But the histology of it suggests that I should already be dead, but I know what's keeping me going, and if that passion, if those two organizations could do this, and if that, as a . . . it's again, you know, "Will there be stars in your crown? Will there be any stars, any stars in your crown?" If there could be, if they could do that, then I would have left something that, in the first case, I am proud of, 'cos I've written so much of it I know, and I've got the same feeling that I had with *Singing Detective* and *Pennies from Heaven*, only even more so, and *Blue Remembered Hills*, that I would go out with a . . . I can now be arrogant and boastful and 'F' it to everything. I could go out with a fitting memorial.

MB: *Thanks a lot.*

DP: That'll have to do. I'm done. I need that thing again, I'm sorry.

MB: *Thank you very much, Dennis. Thanks.*

DP: No. Thank you. You made it easy, Melvyn. But then, you always do. Ta. I felt OK, you see. At certain points, I felt I was flying with it.

MB: *You were.*

DP: And so . . . I'm grateful for the chance. This is my chance to say my last words. So, thanks.

MB: *Thank you.*

DP: Can I finish my drink somewhere?

MB: *Do you want to sit here, or do you want to go to the Green Room, where it's cooler?*

DP: I wouldn't mind getting out of, out of here, to be honest.

MB: *Yeah. No problem. Thanks very much, folks. Thank you. Do you want to come in the Green Room? Thank you very much, everyone.*

The James MacTaggart
Memorial Lecture,
Edinburgh Film Festival,
1993

Relax – or, rather, most of you can – and let us together further dissipate that already minimal level of expectation so appropriate to an occasion such as this.

I am going to propose a deal, thereby starting with the kind of language to which I am, alas, becoming accustomed. The deal is: nobody is allowed to walk out until I finish, except in search of an oxygen mask or a good lawyer. In return, I promise from my side of the autocue that this is not going to be what could properly be called A Lecture, even if it turns out to contain enough recycled material to qualify me for membership of the Liberal Democrat Party, that perennial second prize for those who like to tickle but are afraid to wound.

No, this piece is far more in the nature of a personal statement, or a cry as much from the bile duct as the heart. I recently and profitlessly visited Michael Green, a big man in our business, a personable fellow who must nevertheless be held partly responsible for the predictable disappointment known as Carlton Television. Before going, I checked with a friend of his in red braces how best I could put Mr Green at immediate disadvantage. 'Ask him what he believes in,' the friend said. But I could not bring myself to be quite so cruel.

This evening, however, I insist upon answering that same lethal question for myself. Please accept, therefore, something as ephemeral or self-serving as the ripple of a few pages from what will always remain an unwritten autobiography.

But in order to damp down the smoulder of an individual voice – whose cadences are almost by definition troubling to the mass media – I shall do my level best to pitch these few thousand hastily assembled words at about midpoint between, say, a caterer and a passably humanoid robot, thereby spanning the entire range of what was always somewhat amusingly called independent television and what now in nostalgia only is still occasionally termed 'public service broadcasting'. Maybe I should divert myself by calling this piece 'The Prisoner of Zenda' or better still 'Jurassic Park', but I think they probably need *that* label to pin on the panelled door of the musty room in beleaguered Broadcasting House where, under the puzzled-looking portraits of previous Director-Generals, the ageing, unrepresentative and demonstrably ineffective BBC governors chunter quietly amongst themselves.

Instead, I am giving the melodramatic and not at all tuneful title 'Occupying Powers' to this year's James MacTaggart Memorial Lecture. The title has not been chosen simply to indulge yet again in the inevitable paranoia which so afflicts writers who work in television, although I'll give that a go too. No, I call this 'Occupying Powers' so that I can reflect behind the barricade of metaphor about what it really feels like for many others besides myself who sell their services and some of their passions to the strange new generations of broadcasting managements and their proprietors. More than that, wider than that, I want to use the title 'Occupying Powers' to reach beyond our parochial concerns and grapple with a few thoughts about what it means to be a citizen (or do I mean a consumer?) in the United Kingdom plc, where two-thirds of the population live on incomes below the national average of £250 a week, almost 5¾ million exist on less than £100 a week, 3 million are unemployed, 3 million children live in poverty, one-fifth of the young are innumerate, the chasm between the highest and lowest paid is wider than at any time since 1886, and Dave Lee Travis has resigned from Radio 1. What is at the heart of such a distorted society?

Quote: 'Broadcasting is at the heart of British society. The structure and composition of the broadcasting industry, the purpose and motivation of broadcasters and the programmes and services they offer are vital factors in reflecting and shaping that society.' Unquote. I too would like a mirror that reflects and shapes, but these are the words of the BBC at its most ponderously anodyne as it responded to the government's Green Paper on the future of the Corporation. The ideal colour for this and a few other such BBC replies to the Green Paper should have been a touch more lily-livered or, if you like, lily-liveried in their hues. But the particular quotation is certainly one which James MacTaggart would have taken for granted with as little sense of astonishment as if someone on an outside consultancy contract had told him on three identical bits of thermal paper that a walk along the corridors of the Television Centre will always bring you back shaken but not stirred to where you started.

Jimmy was my first drama producer at the BBC. He was in charge of *Vote, Vote, Vote for Nigel Barton*, the first play of mine to be hoicked off the screen without so much as a by-your-leave on the very day it was scheduled to be broadcast. Believe me, I have by now acquired enough experience of senior television executives to know the exact medical circumstances in which it would be pointless to carry out a spinal tap. But at least a few prominent people at the BBC had by that time moved a trifle closer to the demotic in the spoken if not the written word, and the then Head of Drama appeared to be so troubled by the play's outrageous implication that some party politicians were from time to time on nodding terms with overt cynicism that he asked me why I wanted 'to shit on the Queen'. He must already have known that this is not a particularly easy thing to do from a kneeling position.

These things were happening way back in 1965 in the days of supposedly frequent and untroubled sexual intercourse, the not entirely dissimilar 'white heat of technology' as promised by Harold Wilson (another long-winded way of saying 'fuck you') and the rather slower burn of the Wednesday Play.

Jimmy MacTaggart and his bushy-tailed acolytes used to sit around somewhere in the Fifth Circle talking with a younger conviction about the evident iniquities of the BBC management, the tapeworm-length persistence of BBC cowardice, and the insufferable perversities of the BBC threat to the very existence of the single play. You can imagine how much greater our indignation would have been had we known at the time that we were sitting slap in the middle of what later observers were to call the Golden Age of television drama.

Back in those good old days there was a bureaucrat in every cupboard and smugness waiting with a practised simper on the far side of every other door. I recall these things in order to offer up at least one small strip of sticking plaster for the suppurating wounds of the poor wretch who is the present Director-General, the twelfth and not actually the thirteenth to hold such an exalted (if fully taxable) position at 'the heart of British society'.

I haven't made this long journey in order to be kind and gentle, but I think it is only fair to tell him that the fear and loathing now swirling jugular-high around those same circular corridors do have some antecedents, and it always was possible to measure the distance between so-called management and the so-called creative by the time it took for a memo to go in one direction and a half-brick to come back in the other.

There are a few of us old soldiers still around who know that the best way to polish our campaign medals is to spit on them. I am not blaming John Birt for that particular remark by the way; it was, I believe, attributed to a BBC spokesperson, and since it was immediately comprehensible, I assume it was not made by Mr Birt himself.

It is a wretched thing to have to say, and certain not disinterested newspapers have made it more difficult to say, but it is a fact, known by my own experience and without the faintest possibility of doubt, that there are legions of troubled and embittered employees at the BBC who can scarcely understand any of the concepts of the new 'management culture' which the present and so often so unfairly abused Director-General tries to enunciate. I will willingly concede that this is partly because they do not want to listen, and there have long been people at the BBC ready to spout about their dedication to public service broadcasting who think it is an absolute impertinence if they are asked to get out of their beds of a morning.

I have just this week finished a co-production with the BBC, on which many BBC staff worked as the biggest part of the Corporation's contribution to the budget. The film we made is called, perhaps prophetically enough, *Midnight Movie*, something which in my totally unbiased opinion was brilliantly directed by Renny Rye, who will one day be seen to be one of the great names in British cinema. It is by now part of my job to find and then to support such people, but I would rather have fulfilled this proper obligation without using quite so much of my own money. Unfortunately, *Midnight Movie* was not about a one-legged dwarf with an enormous cock and certain understandable priapic problems and so, perhaps wisely, the properly cautious people who run that near-quango called British Screen could not help me with the budget. And so, naturally I was very pleased when Mark Shivas at the BBC put his shoulder to the boulder that more accurately represents the British film industry than the comparatively minor task of poor Sisyphus.

But it was during the making of *Midnight Movie* that I came to see just how deeply and how seriously the demoralization, the bitterness and, yes, even the hatred had bitten into the working lives of so many hitherto reasonably contented and undoubtedly talented BBC staff. My worst experience was seeing a middle-aged man on the far edge of the set start to cry after a phone call from some manager at the Centre, a grief that I am only marginally glad to say was nothing to do with my script.

I tell you now, it was impossible not to wonder how on earth those currently and I hope temporarily in charge of the BBC could have brought things to such a miserably demeaning condition. My impression was that there is now a one-way system of communication, and that the signals being sent down the narrowed track were so laden with costive, blurb and bubble-driven didacticism that they were more than half perceived as emanating in a squeak of static from someone or, rather, some*thing* alien and hostile. And you cannot make a pair of croak-voiced Daleks appear benevolent even if you dress one of them in an Armani suit and call the other Marmaduke.

A smile can be twisted out of the least promising material, especially when it does not immediately affect oneself. Rather like one of those Marks & Spencer packs that says 'serves two' – make sure that one of you has already eaten first. When making *Midnight Movie*, and watching and listening to what is going on at the BBC as it trims down its staff almost as fast as it loses its viewers, I was struck – and not for the first time – by how much the shifts and turns which seem particular to any one large institution can in themselves be seen as a model for the wider society in which all of us live. Any virulently new 'management culture' can be studied as scrupulously as one might examine the bacteria proliferating around a wound. Both are the response to previous damage made worse by infection picked up from the outside world: the ideas in the unclean air, so to speak. The glories of privatization and the brutalities of the unshackled market – as unleashed by Mrs Thatcher and her successor ideologists – were always likely to rattle a few of the professions, and sometimes rightly so. This genuine radicalism, rare in British politics, can more or less honestly hold up the battle-banners of its occasionally healthy and often vicious indifference to the old, class-ridden, status-conscious cultures of Great

Britain. This iconoclasm fractured many old attitudes, many old bonds and even many whole communities. The cry of Yuppie to Yuppie sounded in the land, as chilling as any call from the carnivores in swamp or forest. And the deep hatred of any other claim, any other way of seeing, of anything other than the forces of law and order in the public domain, was always going to be arrowed with poison-dipped barb at the slow, decent, stumbling and puzzled giant run from Broadcasting House.

And thus it is in model form that the turmoil, the distress, the dogma-driven rhetoric, the obtuseness and the spluttering aggressions at and around the BBC can also be picked up in similar shapes, cries, contortions and an almost identical bluster – from *both* sides – in so many other areas of our national life. We have been at war with each other, and some of our fellow citizens have felt that bits of their very brain and fibres from their very soul are being crunched with the other, apparently all-important numbers in the computer. No wonder that, out there, there is talk of moral panic, and a sense that our feet are scrambling about on loose scree.

Moral panic? Loose scree? Any moment now I shall be talking like a newspaper editorial. May the shades of this Kirk protect me from such ignominy. But let me gently slide in the needle at this point to inject one of those psychotropic reagents that can for a while stimulate into strange new activity a previously slumbering cluster of brain cells. I am looking to find the kind of juxtaposition that most economically tells a tale. And here's one worth thinking about.

At the time Rupert Murdoch was anxiously trying to gild if not renovate his image while lobbying to prevent his cable television company coming under the same rules and regulations that apply to other British television companies, he announced that his main company was going to fund a new chair at Oxford University to the tune of £3 million. It was to be called the – I do beg your pardon, but I cannot keep a straight face – it was to be called the Murdoch Chair in Language and Communications. But the announcement came with cack-handed timing on the very same day that the Press Council formally, and of course ineffectively, censured Murdoch's *Sun* for calling homosexuals 'poofters'. Some language. Some communication. Murdoch did not turn up for the ceremonial meal to mark the largesse at Oxford, always a place where the gap between the cup and the lip can be measured by more than an inch of the sardonic. But Rupert has a touch of pure cruelty in his make-up. He sent Kelvin MacKenzie, the sharp little weasel that edits that daily stink they call the *Sun*, and the maladroit fellow had to sit and chew and probably even dribble a bit between two professors. Well, that was one set of cutlery not needed on the crisp linen, I suppose. But I hope for the sake of all concerned that both the professors were from the Anthropology faculty.

The reason I am speaking in this way on this occasion is not simply because my fists are already clenched, and not just because I really do want to land a few blows on some of the nastiest people besmirching our once-fair land. No, it is because I object to the manner in which too many of us too much of the time half hide behind the anonymous, the over-smoothed, over-soothed and anodyne. Even as we quietly rot or noisily spin, and even as the disaffected, the dispossessed, the poor and the more than half-mad surge almost necessarily unnoticed at the littered edges of the gutters, even then, even then, the normal, polite metalanguage of Britspeak and its half-way decent conceptual evasions, modulated only by a whine, choke off enough of the pain or sufficient of the venom. But then we are left emptied of almost everything except a numbing bewilderment, a paralysis of the spirit, and that long, aching, nearly inexpressible sense of *loss* which is, I feel – what's the current phrase? – the 'hidden agenda' lurking behind so much of our public discourse, with something of the same stretched rictus of proper embarrassment in which a former Labour Chancellor of the Exchequer currently fronts a few TV commercials. Embarrassment. Well, it's a fluttery enough, flustered enough word to take me now into a long loop all the way back to the blue remembered hills of my own childhood. You will have to excuse what might at first seem to be a self-indulgent digression but I need to make this journey to gather up a few of the things I want to say. Somewhere back there is the set of reasons or feelings for why I wanted to place my work on to the palace of varieties in the corner of the living room rather than first of all between the covers of a book or on the theatre stage. A critic on the *Guardian* has said, with a neat little edge of ambivalence, that for thirty years I have shown a fidelity to television which would astonish a Labrador retriever. I'm not always sure that I can tell one dog from another, but I have to say that if I were starting out today as a writer who is able to persuade himself on at least two days of the week that drama or fiction is one of the last few remaining acres of possible truth-telling left to us in our over-manipulated and news-stuffed world, then I doubt very much that I would deliberately choose, as I did, to begin in television as it is now controlled, owned and organized. But let me go back a bit. Beam me up, Scottie, or down, if not quite to the Land of Lost Content.

My first home was in the Forest of Dean, which rises steeply in ever tighter layers of green and grey in what is purely coincidentally a heart-shaped mound between the Severn and the Wye, close to the border with Wales. I was four years old when the Second World War began, and it took me until I was ten before I finally won it, with a little help from Rockfist Rogan, Tommy Handley and Mr Harris at Salem Chapel. In those days, the main sources of work in the district were the five deep-shaft coal-mines, long since closed, and the stone quarries, whose rumbling explosions made me wonder if the Germans were coming. My father worked with pick and shovel on the pre-mechanized coal-face, and most of the men in the village worked in the same colliery. The school, long since abandoned, had windows too high for a child to look out of, gravestones of dead foresters right up to its back wall and a big locked cupboard of books – *real* books (!) – and how to break into it after hours was for me an avid but wholly secretive preoccupation which, if only I had had the courage to put into reality might well have begun the passage into just sufficient criminality and bad faith to allow me in later years to write a television franchise application.

The forest had long been fairly isolated from everywhere else – *even Wales* – and between the boundaries of the two rivers it had become almost suffocatingly in-turned. The speech, for example, was so broad, so full of forgotten English and so buttered with 'thee' and 'thou' and the 'highsht' which was 'hist', or listen-with-urgency, or the 'surry' which was 'sirrah', that it could almost be said to be a dialect. 'Where bist thou a-going, o'butty?' 'It chunt as I cont, surry – it's just as I byunt' or 'Doosn't thou start gewling at me, mind, else I shall sort tha' out!' An almost test-tube perfect case for assessing the impact of the mass media, the motives of those who own it and the consequences for the people who experience it.

There it was: the pit, the chapel, the brass band, the rugby team, the speech. I don't know how to explain this to you. I don't know how to make you understand. It was tempered or maybe diminished for me by the fact that my mother was a Londoner, the daughter of a Forest of Dean woman who had gone into what was called domestic service – that is, being a skivvy – in the distant capital and who had exchanged that near-slavery for the drudgery of marrying a Hammersmith plumber and bringing up ten other children beside my mother in a variety of rented and mostly terraced houses. My mother came to the Forest of Dean on a weekend charabanc trip to visit her strangely spoken and flushless-toileted relatives, and was duly impressed by my father's ever-shy little smile, gentle little delicacies, sparkling well-polished shoes and, most importantly of all, perhaps, the way he sang 'I'm painting the clouds with sunshine', with an emphatic if hardly necessary double stamp-stamp of those same well-polished feet to mark each otherwise wistful chorus. Jesus, my throat narrows. You are not supposed to talk like this in our country. *When I hold back a tear/To let a smile appear/I'm only painting/The clouds – with sunshine* ...

Would someone with a hard face please protect me from those sickly and sugared old tunes? They tinkle-tinkle their simple sweetness and yet somehow complicated accusations out of the most personally demeaning residues of what had seemed to be lost and gone for ever. I'm fairly sure as a soiled adult slowly disintegrating into advanced middle age that it is salutary for each one of us to look back on our own past with more than a degree of tender contempt. But there are a few still-lingering and probably still-mocking syncopations which can remind us, however faintly, however ambiguously, that the usual deadening materiality of *things out there*, or the insistent present tense of the implacably busy world, is other than just what we see. There is too a 'wonder' in and of our shrunken mortality and our scrabbling appetites which maybe prayer and maybe drama and maybe just a song or a dance or a breeze in the air can sometimes fleetingly catch hold of. That is why, as I bent over the blank page, I allowed Arthur Parker, the haplessly dishonest and helplessly adulterous sheet-music salesman in *Pennies from Heaven* to lift his head in pained recognition as 'Painting the Clouds with Sunshine' throbbed along to middle-eight and because he was better than he seemed – or wanted to be – and knew in some part of his tawdry soul that those wisps of song were chariots of grace, like the Psalms of David. And then I hanged him.

Or, rather, that was what was supposed to happen in the last few pages of a six-part script which I am sure in my own mind was only commissioned because a few people at the BBC felt just a little guilty about the banning of my *Brimstone and Treacle* in the previous twelve months. That's the way things used to work – a smack and then a kiss. The then and new Head of Drama looked at the scripts, listened to me talk, shuffled a bit in his sockless sandals and then asked with the faintest tinge of alarm or incredulity. 'What? You mean they pretend to sing in every episode?'

But, as I say, I never did get to see Arthur Parker descend through the trap door on the studio-designed scaffold. The clock had ticked on in the final studio session and exactly, but exactly, on the hour, just as Bob Hoskins had swallowed in his no doubt suddenly dried throat, the BBC sparks pulled the plug. Sorry, guv, and all that sort of stuff, which was *also* part of the old BBC, no matter how many times you hear the word 'dedication' from the union side in the current brouhaha at the Corporation.

But 'Painting the Clouds' has, of course, tempted me off track. It was sung in an England where everyone was supposed to know his place, and it felt like it too, no matter what the song. I grew up and grew away in that English manner from kith and kin whose talents had been so long unused that they were now all but unusable. It began to seem to me, with the sly whispers of academic success in my ear, that their expectations had been made to shrink to little more than the width of the room. Our own land was in the hands of others, and these others were not interested in our growth, or emancipation. And that is what defines an occupying power .

But when I said just now in the exaggerations of rhetoric that aspirations were scarcely wider than the spaces between the parlour walls, I was leaving out the one big window, and it wasn't the one made of glass. We called it, then, the wireless. A whorled, fluted and beknobbed oblong which could allow anyone to feel like Joan of Arc.

More than the coming of the bus and the train, or even the daily newspaper, it was the voices out of the air which, as though by magic, pushed out those constricting boundaries. You could hear a play that made the back of your neck tingle as well as a dance band that made your foot tap, a brow-furrowing talk about something I'd never heard of, as well as an I-say-I-say-I-say music-hall routine, or even (and how bizzare) a ventriloquist's dummy as well as a not wholly dissimilar newsreader. And none of it was trying to sell you anything. Maybe.

I would not dispute for one wayward whistle or crackle that the BBC of my childhood was not paternalistic and often stuffily pompous. It saw itself in an almost priestly role. But at a crucial period of my life it threw open the 'magic casement' on great sources of mind-scape at a time when books were hard to come by, and when I had never stepped into a theatre or a concert hall, and would have been scared to do so even if given the chance.

Of course, the characteristic media ploy of separating the 'popular' from the 'serious' – which often means the distinction between the solemn and the lively, and not just the truncheon-like measuring rod of class and educational status – of course, yes, that process had already begun with the split between the Home Service and the Light Programme. But such a parting of the ways was nothing like as rigidly mapped out as it is nowadays, where listeners are presumed to be walking about with one of the digits One to Five tattooed like cattle brands on their high, middling, low, lower and yet lower brows. On the old Light Programme you could suddenly, maybe reluctantly, collide with a play or a discussion or an embryonic drama-documentary. The now totally pervasive assumptions of the market-place, which have stiffened into something close to natural law, had not by then removed the chance of being surprised by something you didn't know, or – better still – by something you didn't know that you knew.

When there is a certain type of functionary on the other and more powerful side of the desk, or when faced with a particular kind of audience, I'll admit that I'm quite ready to be a churl in sharpened hobnails, as I hope to show a little later this evening. But it would be graceless of me not to acknowledge with an open heart the significant part the BBC had played in my life and in the lives of the people I came from. Millions of our fellow citizens feel the same way, for there have been all too few British institutions of any size of which one could say with hand on heart that they truly work, that they are the 'best' that is.

I place quotation marks around 'best' because the potential vices of any form of moderated paternalism are all too clear, and were too often demonstrated in the old BBC monopoly, first and for longest in radio and then for many years in television. Paternalism has been defined as power with a conscience, and it can also be arrogance without a banana skin. This-is-what-we-think-is-good-for-you sounds much too much like that wretched hospital the other week which allowed a patient to die rather than modulate its little package of prejudice.

The dangers of the older view of how to run radio and television are, unless faced and redefined, sufficiently troubling to leave enough space for someone such as Rupert Murdoch to drive a golden coach and a team of wild-eyed horses straight through the gap. His James MacTaggart Lecture here a few years ago was little short of a masterpiece of apparently libertarian rhetoric. Indeed, it was the kind of peroration I would like to hear him deliver from the scaffold.

The insecurities and contradictions of the BBC's only half-digested and half-shamefaced self-definitions lay like rubble spread in inviting heaps in front of the supercharged, savage-toothed JCB of his unslaked appetite. The Corporation has already been driven on to the back foot by the ideology-driven malice of the ruling politicians, and its response has been to take several more steps backwards, with hands thrown up, and to whimper an alleged defence of all it has stood for in the very language and concepts of its opponents. This palpable ambivalence and doubt, where you pretend to be the commercial business that you cannot be, has led to the present, near-fatal crisis where it seems to be thought that the wounds (often self-afflicted) can only be staunched by shuffling about word-processed words about a new 'management culture'.

Management of what? Management for what? Management. Management. Management. The word sticks in one's interface. Please excuse me if I dare to laugh, but I know that each age, even each decade, has its little cant word coiled up inside real discourse like a tiny grub in the middle of an apple. Each age, even each decade, is overly impressed for a little while by half-way bright youngish men on the make who adeptly manipulate the current terminology at precisely the right moment to make precisely the right impression on those who are a little older, a little less intelligent and considerably less alert. Ah, me! Which one of us here this evening has not fallen into one or other of these categories, and perhaps into the wrong one at the very moment we thought we were in the other? Life in the media business can be a hoot.

As a writer who needs to clutch his pen as though it were a lifebelt, I have to admit that I have nevertheless improved many a shining hour with a probably untransmittable little playlet about one of the more intriguing encounters of our time. I was not there when Fortnum met Mason, Laurel met Hardy, or Murdoch met Mephistopheles, but I would have given my old *Thesaurus* or my new sequence of Reader's Digest Prize Draw Numbers to have been a hornet on the wall at that surely entrancing, fascinating and maybe even comical occasion when dear old Marmaduke first met dear young John and each of them sort of half discussed what was sort of half wrong with the greatest broadcasting organization the world has ever seen. Where, I wonder, did they meet? Who was the first to smile – lethally? Who said, 'structural walk-through' as he ordered the mineral water? And did the waiter say, 'Pardon?'

Was the table well laden and did it groan when the unadvertised post of the twelfth and not the thirteenth Director-Generalship was finally settled? And were the ageing governors at the British Broadcasting Corporation waiting and twitching and nodding amongst themselves in some cramped little area decently set aside at the front of the room where you deposit your hats, coats, tightly furled umbrellas and maybe, in the case of one of them, your spare 'Honk If You Love Jesus' car-stickers.

My invention has not run out, and it might be nice to go in this vein, so indelicately poised at midpoint between farce and malice, but the temptation to dish back what has been so wantonly dished out must be resisted. After all, a laugh has such a close psychological resemblance to a scream of outrage, so what I ought to do in the concluding sections of this piece is to put the polemic on the back burner, where it can ooze and bubble away into a very nice soup that we can all taste later. And with long spoons, if need be.

It is too easy to accuse others of betrayal when you are not ready to acknowledge your own. I remember the way in which I made the journey up the tick-tick-tick examination ladder, all the way to Oxford. Teachers love to get their hands on a bright and pliant child, and they do not consciously give wing to the invisible worm that flies in the night, bringing the blight of an especially English type of betrayal deep into the oh-look-at-me! folds of the most precocious bloom. You are first made to feel a little different, and then you *want* to be different; and although you know what you gain with your little Latin and less Greek, you do not for a long time realize what you have lost.

The glittering prizes are there all right, as they always have been for a few – and not all of those few can be described as 'stout of heart'. Glitter, glitter little star, how seldom we wonder what you are! But when a little of the sheen sticks to your own eager fingers or glints in your own deliberately wide eyes, you soon come to use the refractive light to see into the cosy and otherwise secretive little corners where those with real power smile so affably at each other. I soon enough came to know in the Oxford of the fifties that those beautiful spires are not so much dreaming as *calculating*. It took an indecently short time for me to decide to become a politician – and that was only partly because I wanted to open for others the doors which had been opened for me.

I had developed a superficially astonishing ability to be, as tonight, eloquent, aggressive and sanctimonious all at one and the same time, as well as the useful knack of smiling with my mouth only in what must have been an instinctive rehearsal for a future hypothetical question. Hell, and I *mean* hell, I could fairly easily have mutated into a marginally more charming version of – of – No. No. No names. This is a Kirk. The devil will surely claim me. Tick one of many boxes and pick a name for yourself. But, yes, I sensed, once, that a laurel-edged path was opening up invitingly at my feet and I knew that it would lead to upholstered media power, or to a padded bench not too far from the mace in Parliament, or a padded cell somewhere not at all dissimilar but even more interesting, wearing a jacket that buttons up at the back.

Instead, and in what I now see as a mysterious act of grace, I had what must be a version of a middle course chosen for me, and very soon after coming down from New College I finished up in hospital scarcely able to move. An entropy of the spirit, I suppose, manifest in the swollen rigidities of each limb and the fiercely scalding mockery of their outer casing.

And so it was that thirty or more years ago, apparently stripped of much more than my skin, I had the opportunity of reassembling myself from what I hesitate to call scratch. I had the chance of making myself up all over again.

This interesting and intrinsically dramatic process not only restored to me a sufficient measure of dignity but also had the immeasurable advantage, in due time, of giving me what I have to call a sense of vocation, if you will pardon me such an antique phrase.

My condition was genetic, but it felt psychological. I knew that I had lost touch with something, and that the soapbox words were no longer capable of restoring enough of what had been half-unknowingly jettisoned. Different words had to be found, with different functions and a different purpose. But how? And why? *Why-Why-Why?* The same desperately repeated question I had asked myself without any sort of answer, or any ability to tell my mother or my father, when, at the age of ten, between VE day and VJ day, I had been trapped by an adult's sexual appetite and abused out of innocence. If anyone cares to look, really look, at my work over the years, they would not take too long to see how the great bulk of it is about the victim, someone who cannot explain, cannot put into the right words, or even cannot speak at all. But I do know, without doubt, that the nearer writing approaches self-therapy, the worse it becomes. As I have just said, but now in a shifted context, different words had to be found, with different functions. But how? What used to be weeks in hospital then stretched into months in hospital, but still the language would not break itself open. The love of my family, and the steadfastness of my wife Margaret, in particular, became for a long while the only or major defence against a near-total reclusiveness. This is, of course, before chemotherapy lifted the bondage, providing a large degree of emancipation at the price of intermittent liver biopsies and a regular up-chuck time that seemed entirely fitting for one who had for too long, and with a dangerously religious temperament, felt that the only truly meaningful sacrament left was for people to gather at the mud-died and unlit crossroads at eventide in order to vomit. Collec-tively.

All right. This is getting too extreme. It is becoming embar-rassing. You should not ask a writer to deliver one of these pieces, because too many of you too much of the time are paid not to let anything remotely resembling real emotions or *real writing* get anywhere near anything other than weary-sigh-distance of your so regularly emptied out-trays. But don't shuffle and fret. Just look upon this as a day out, as you might a trip to the zoo.

In any form of personal crisis, all kinds of memory and aspiration, hope and disappointment, grief and bloody-mindedness fly up at you as suddenly and as startlingly as the little yellowhammer bird used to do from the prickly gorse-bushes of boyhood. And in that unbidden mix, as though out of a fever, I began at last, and seriously, to make links that I had studiously or even furtively avoided making for too long.

'Only connect,' said E. M. Forster, that great novelist whom Murdoch's nasty little rag would presumably dismiss as an artsy-fartsy old poofter. But, yes, what a good word: *connect*. The verb which far better than the merely technical *transmit* is, if not actually, certainly what should be the defining activity of all television – especially that threatened and peculiarly *self*-threatened section which has no need, and indeed no remit, to package up A-, B- or C-defined groups of the allegedly passive on behalf of predatory advertisers. The section of broadcasting which, above all else, and quite separately from any temporarily dominant political language or so-called 'management culture', must continually remind itself that it is *not* a business trying to distribute dosh to its shareholders, *not* owned by its current administrators, *not* a company entitled to build Chinese walls around its momentary practices, but something held in trust and in law for every citizen of this misgoverned and too-long abused group of nations we, for probably a few decades more, call Great Britain and Northern Ireland.

I have already described with real gratitude how the radio days of my childhood widened the horizons, and sometimes made them shimmer. Those plummy voices spoke as though from another land, and yet they did not seem to be trying to make one a stranger in it, let alone a shopper. I think, even, that they were *trusted*, unlike virtually all the other manifestations of power and authority. But perhaps this was partly due to the fact that you could not see the pictures, and radio people too often quote with pride the child who so famously said that she preferred the radio to television 'because the scenery is better'.

Television could scarcely resist calling itself 'a window on the world', as it did in its early days, even using the subtitle on *Panorama*. But windows have frames, and the frames are part of a structure that has already been built. I have said, many years ago, that on the television screen it is often when the set is switched off that it actually picks up a direct or true reflection of its viewers, subdued into a glimmer on its dull grey tube. When the set is on, alive with images, the window analogy persists because, away from the expensive brilliance and often genuine sophistication of title sequences, logos and the commercials, most of television, most TV journalism, most of its decidedly over-long news programmes, all of its proliferating soaps, most of its dramas, pretend or assume or wish that the picture in the frame – adjusted for a laugh, a snigger, a gasp or a tear – is showing us things as they really are.

So-called naturalism is by far and away the dominant mode,

and easily the most characteristic syntax of television grammar. But one of the troubles of supposedly showing things-as-they-really-are (the window problem) is how difficult it then becomes in the same grammar not to make people feel deep in their souls that this is also more or less the way things have to be. Hence the shock-horror-probe patterns, the inflated status of those bus conductors called news readers, the odd and only temporarily effective splashes of sensational indignation, the random violence, the unmediated sexuality, and the presence of critics who almost uniformly perceive their function to be joke-makers and snide-mongers. Who can blame them?

Our television has been ripped apart and falteringly reassembled by politicians who believe that value is a monetary term only, and that a cost-accountant is thereby the most suitable adjudicator of what we can and cannot see on our screens. And these accountants or their near-clones are employed by new kinds of media owners who try to gobble up everything in their path. We must protect ourselves and our democracy, first by properly exercising the cross-ownership provisions currently in place, and then by erecting further checks and balances against dangerous concentrations of the media power which plays such a large part in our lives. No individual, group or company should be allowed to own more than one daily, one evening and one weekly newspaper. No newspaper should be allowed to own a television station, and vice versa. A simple act of public hygiene, tempering abuse, widening choice, and maybe even returning broadcasting to its makers.

The political pressures from market-obsessed radicals, and the huckster atmosphere that follows, have by degrees, and in confused self-defence, drawn the BBC so heavily into the dogma-coated discourses of so-called 'market efficiency' that in the end it might lose clear sight of why it, the BBC, is there in the first place.

I fear the time is near when we must save not the BBC from itself but public service broadcasting from the BBC. The old Titan should spawn smaller and more nimble offspring if its present controllers cannot be removed. Why not think about it anyway? Why not separate radio from television? Why not let BBC2 be a separate public service broadcaster? Let us begin to consider afresh how the thousands of millions of pounds of licence money could be apportioned between two, three or four successors to the currently misled Corporation. One of the successors could certainly be a publishing or commissioning authority on the model of Channel 4.

Indeed, Channel 4, if freed from its advertisements, could continue to evolve out of its original, ever-precious remit into a passably good model of the kinds of television some of us seek. Michael Grade is becoming, by default, the new Director-General, and the ironies, if not the comedy, of such an unexpected grace remind me that it is time to wind down before I exhaust myself with my own restraint.

Thirty years ago, under the personal pressures of whatever guilt, whatever shame and whatever remaining shard of idealism, I found or I made up what I may unwisely have termed a sense of vocation. I have it still. It was born, of course, from the already aborted dream of a common culture which has long since been zapped into glistening fragments by those who are now the real, if not always recognized, occupying powers of our culture. Look in the pink pages and see their mesh of connections. Open the *Sun* and measure their aspirations. Put Rupert Murdoch on public trial and televise every single second of it. Show us who is abusing us, and why. Ask your public library – if there is one left – to file the television franchise applications on the shelf hitherto kept for Fantasy, Astrology and Crime bracket Bizarre bracket.

I was exceptionally fortunate to begin my career in television at a time when the BBC was so infuriatingly confident about what public service broadcasting meant that the question itself was not even on what would now be called the agenda. The then ITV companies shared much more of this ethos than they were then willing to acknowledge. Our profession was then mostly filled with men and women who mostly cared about the programmes rather than the dividend. And the venomous hostilities of the small minority who are the political right – before its wholly ideological transformation into the type of venal, wet-mouthed radicalism which can even assert without a hint of shame that 'there is no such thing as society' – before those people had yet launched their poisoned arrows. Clunk! they go. Clunk! Clunk! And, lo and behold, we have in the fullness of such darkness sent unto us a Director-General who bares his chest to receive these arrows, a St Sebastian eager for their punishing stings.

The world has turned upside-down. The BBC is under governors who seem incapable of performing the public trust that is invested in them, under a Chairman who seems to believe he is heading a private fiefdom, and under a Chief Executive who must somehow or other have swallowed whole and unsalted the kind of humbug-punctuated pre-privatization manual which is being forced on British Rail or British Coal. But I do not want to end on a malediction. Let me remind myself of how to paint the clouds with sunshine. I first saw television when I was in my late teens. It made my heart *pound.* Here was a medium of great power, of potentially wondrous delights, that could slice through all the tedious hierarchies of the printed word and help to emancipate us from many of the stifling tyrannies of class and status and gutter-press ignorance. We are privileged if we can work in this, the most entrancing of all the many palaces of varieties. Switch on, tune in and *grow.*

I hope it is clear by now that I happen to care very much about the medium that has both allowed and shaped the bulk of my life's work, and even my life's meaning. However, I do have the odd hour or two in each day in which to pretend to be a St George rather than a St Sebastian. I therefore hereby formally apply in front of witnesses of substance, here at the Edinburgh International Television Festival, for the post of Chairman of the Governors of the British Broadcasting Corporation.

An interview with Alan Yentob, BBC2, 1987

ALAN YENTOB: *Looking back at your work over the past twenty years or so, there are a startling number of themes which are either revisited or redrawn throughout that period. How far are you fuelled today by the same obsessions as then? Do you feel about them as you did when you first began to write?*

DENNIS POTTER: I think any writer who keeps going over a couple of decades or so is going to be ploughing the same stretch of land whether he knows it or not. In fact, you don't know it until much later on and then you not only know it, you welcome it because you don't ever plough the land properly and you're always – there's always the possibility that some coin, or some richness that you didn't know that you knew, is there, waiting to be turned up the next plough round. I don't see that I'm ever going to get off that plough or wheel or whatever it is, because that is the thing that makes me a writer and stops me not being a writer.

In other words, I wouldn't rest if I thought that there was still another turn to make in the same field.

AY: *How did you come to write at all? Why did you decide to write?*

DP: I don't know, I don't think anyone decides to write, you just find that you are writing. I had thought that I was going to be a politician, I'd thought that my . . . that the instinct that I knew I had, and didn't understand what that instinct was, was going to lead me into politics because that seemed to be the access to what it was I wanted to say. In fact it isn't and wasn't.

But I was, as a working-class child – I had a high IQ. I learned to read before I went to school – in the chapel, for example, on the Sundays, which used to be Salem Chapel up the hill – clean shoes, clean hanky and all those dreadful, you

59

know, you mustn't use four-letter words, hymns come rolling out over you, and which, one of the things I remember was the pencil – writing a hymn. And again my mother taking it from me with some worry, because it was a wet day, and saying, 'What sort of boy are you going to turn into?' as it were, because you are writing bloody hymns. Fair enough, I'd wop my child if I found it doing it. But it was that – I knew that the words were chariots in some way. I didn't know where it was going, or what release and/or torment it might lead to, but it was so inevitable. That's why I have difficulty in answering questions about why or what and when did you become a writer. Because I cannot think of the time really when I wasn't in one way or another.

AY: *So you were attracted by the language that you heard in the church, and by the sentiments as well?*

DP: No, I wasn't attracted by the language. Initially I thought that that was the language of imaginative discourse and the stories – I don't know if you ever remember Hazlitt's description of his father reading the Bible? When I read that, I recognized the same feel and strength of it, that the images of the Bible, the sand and the Valley of the Shadow of Death, or Jacob wrestling with the angel – I knew exactly where that was. I knew where the Valley of the Shadow of Death was, which was a lane overhung with trees behind the village where I used to whistle, as you went down it, because in – say, on a winter's dusk, you know, which would be the time you would be coming home from school . . . Now I have always associated the Chapel language with that terrible withdrawal of light at about three and four o'clock in the afternoon on a November, December schoolday, and when my father died in 1975 on a November day, exactly the same, and I felt then – that's what I felt as a child, I felt that feeling, that terrible, emptying out of . . . that you were wriggling on a pin and there was nothing and no one was going to lift you off it and the light was being sucked out of the sky, and there were these terrible words rolling around you.

AY: *The* Beast with Two Backs *seems to be a play very much about the people and the spirit of the Forest of Dean. I mean it has a historical setting in the nineteenth century but it has an almost feudal flavour in its atmosphere. It's where you come from, of course, and you've drawn on it a great deal throughout your work. But what is it that is so particular about it, about the Forest of Dean?*

DP: The villagers had their origins entirely in coal-mining, and the pits were like great black sows buried in the trees; and all the villages were mining villages, and therefore are not English country villages – there were no squires.

You said feudal, you see I don't – you see the Forest of Dean isn't like that. It isn't like, say, the Sussex village or – it's both more democratic and more powerful in its emotions within the villages than the word 'feudal' might suggest.

And I suppose using the *Beast with Two Backs* was a way of nodding at some of that, or submitting to some of that. And if home is where ... someone said where you start from, then clearly that sort of culture is going to continually send up tremors through me, no matter what I do or where I go.

AY: *But how much did you feel part of it? I mean, you were an extremely clever child – you were set apart from the other children. You've said this yourself. I mean, you've even talked of being humiliated at school. Did you feel different from other children? I mean, did you have a sense of being different?*

DP: Probably, yes. But if I'd been, say – say I'd been better at football, it wouldn't have mattered so much. Or if I'd been less physically cowardly, it wouldn't have mattered so much, but the two things reinforced each other, so that I then became ... when they were filming *The Singing Detective*, for example, in the Forest of Dean, they went there and they found that – I wasn't there on that recce and I vowed don't save me, Jesus Christ, I will not do that – went on that recce and they met some of the people I was brought up with, and they said, 'Oh you were at school with Dennis, were you?' This to a girl whom I well remember, whose name I won't mention, and she said, 'Well, Dennis would never have climbed a tree, because he was too timid.' But of course I did, but only when I was alone. So there was that sense in which I could do anything, and say anything and dare anything, as long as there was no witness, as the witness would have immediately translated it into their terms, terms which I was already uncomfortable about.

So all that warm, suffocating, you know in one sense, interned, insular Forest of Dean, working-class, Chapel, brass band, rugby football, male-voice choir, all that. On one level I wanted to be part of it, and longed for acceptance in it. On another level, I was already beginning to judge it and be the cocky scholarship boy, if you like, who's at the very moment of embracing it, compromising it.

AY: *In 1959, after leaving Oxford University, Potter joined the BBC and worked as a television trainee in the Television Talks Department. Rather surprisingly, he was invited to write and narrate a documentary film about his own life and background even though he was only twenty-four.*

DP: I'd started working for the BBC in September/October 1959 and worked briefly in *Panorama* and then with Denis Mitchell, and then I had the chance because of the way I was a spouter then in best BBC sense, always talking about what I wanted to do, and Grace Wyndham Goldie had this slot and said, 'See what you can do.' That was my first meeting with film cameras and with the BBC at work, as it were – as opposed to television cameras in the studio in the discussion programmes and what have you – and it, well, it fascinated me, the process fascinated me, and the lies fascinated me, and the way in which it failed to deal with what I knew to be there.

AY: *How much of that do you feel was your responsibility?*

DP: Well, a great deal of it. I was what, twenty-three, -four, and it was about my own background, and it trapped me into, I trapped myself into making premature judgements about things that actually were terribly dear and tender to me, which in that way is characteristic of the callow; I was embarrassed by the tenderness of them, and therefore the embarrassment had to be expressed in rhetoric and the rhetoric was phoney, because rhetoric usually is . . . But it was seeing what it is you're observing, seeing how those scenes with the clapperboard in front of them got turned into that, and seeing what was on either side of the camera and wasn't on the film, and the way that my own voice-over had diminished what this person was saying, or what this person was about to say, which is worse. It taught me how easy the betrayal is compared to, using the word in quotes if you like, 'art', which is not concerned with betrayal, and art cannot betray in that sense.

AY: *This concern with betrayal, which is also betrayal of values, betrayal of ideas, is very much there at the beginning of the writing, isn't it? Again going back to that experience of that particular film . . . to some extent did you feel that you'd betrayed your parents, your father?*

DP: Yes, I did.

AY: *And did* Nigel Barton *come out of that?*

DP: To a degree. There was a scene in *Vote, Vote, Vote for Nigel Barton* with the television: he appeared on television and had to watch it with his parents, and that they didn't mind, they were proud of him, but he knew that he'd been a shit, and *mea culpa*, yes.

AY: *What about betrayal when you went into politics yourself? I mean, did you go into it with the notion that this was something that you could be effective in? That there was, that you could support your class, that you could be effective in politics?*

DP: I thought I could be effective in politics, yes, and I was a good speaker and a good Party representative in a safe Conservative seat, so it didn't matter too much. But I, when I went canvassing with my political agent at the time, you know, and the doors, various doors would open and they'd say, 'Can we rely upon your vote?' which is essentially – canvassing is only about making sure that those whom you know support you come out. And then they would start discussing things like, 'What are you going to do about all the blacks?' Well, I would attempt to engage and get a sharp kick on the ankle, which was fair enough, because his job was to get the vote out, and mine was to realize that I was in the wrong trade, and no matter how effective I was as a speaker ... believe me, I felt that very strong streak of charlatanry in me, which made me – I would probably be leader of the Labour Party by now if I hadn't been ill, and ... in other words, I could have been that kind of sub-criminal.

AY: *Much of the drama in your plays is centred round the dilemmas faced by individuals – the dilemmas of self, if you like. They're about paradox and contradiction, about anxieties, and one of the ways in which you explore these themes is through this idea of betrayal. One child betrays another child at school, the betrayal of infidelity, your preoccupation with Burgess and Maclean, patriotism and treason. It's as if the shape of your characters' lives is defined by their failure to live up to their own aspirations; and it also seems the failure of the world to live up to their expectations.*

DP: Well, I don't think it's going too far to say that might actually be the shape of anyone's life. To be at the high tide of belief in anything – if you're capable of believing – most people are at some point in their lives capable of believing in something bigger and more demanding than they think it is, and when it's at high tide, and the sun's on the sea, and there's a mimosa-clad beach, it appears to be the answer to everything, whether it's political belief, religious belief, or personal commitment like falling in love, say, it would appear to be both a high moment and 'the answer', in quotes. But inevitably and humanly, as your own body betrays you as you age, so the purity, for example, of a political belief can be fortunately temporized by your own commitments, your own laziness, your own dealing with the rough and tumble of life – which saves people from becoming ideologues, if you like. And the passionate priest/politician is dangerous, because the high tide is still drumming in his head and ears. But the falling away of belief, and the falling away of commitment, while partly inevitable, still tears – where those beliefs stuck to you, it still tears away the flesh from the bone, metaphorically speaking.

You cannot betray and be comfortable with the betrayal, and it's pointing out or observing or charting, not with any didactic sense but merely observing it, that can give some of the spring and tension in the drama.

AY: *You, of course, abandoned your own political ambition after the 1964 election and decided to write. You could have written for the theatre, you could have written novels, but you didn't; you chose to write for television. Why did you decide that?*
DP: I had the ... yearning, maybe – I don't know what is the right word to use for there to be a possibility at least of a common culture. I don't think that way, in quite the same way now. But then it was much more plausible to think in those terms, with just the two channels, and then I'd chosen television partly to assuage some guilt, if you like, or anxieties. But also because the same instinct that wanted me, that made me want to be a Labour politician was not in order that the Party should prosper or that I should get elected to Parliament – although, of course, that was part and parcel of it – but it was really

something else which was like being in primary school again and making everything all right ... which was that all sorts and conditions of human being could share the same experiences, do share the same experiences, and that because of the tyranny and treachery of words, which are dependent upon education, which in itself is dependent upon class in England – that one of the ways of jumping over the hierarchies of the print culture was television, because anyone or everyone could see it.

AY: *So obviously the democracy of television appealed to you, but you broke the rules right from the word go. You started to confound the formal conventions of television. In* Nigel Barton, *for instance, you first started to use children as adults – something that you did later on in* Blue Remembered Hills. *What did you learn from this process of writing* Nigel Barton?

DP: I learned from it how far I had to go. But I also learned that you could do it. And that by making what appeared to be – because they didn't appear to me to be innovations, that was the point, I thought how is it that I'm going to express it. How is it, for example, if you are describing the behaviour of children, how is it, how are you going to communicate both the excitement, the zest, the terror, the anxiety, the whatever, the whatever of the relationship between those children to an adult audience? The only way it seemed to me to make it really possible was not to allow the adult to distance himself or herself by saying, 'Ahh, children', how, a twee distancing, the wrong sort of alienating effect, if you like, but it was to show how awful or how marvellous or whatever, how whatever it was by making them adult. But at the same time using the adult body as the magnifying glass for the childhood, of physicality in childhood, emotion in childhood, restlessness, but using that as the reverse of the magnifying glass as well, to make you see how much of it was still in adult life.

AY: *There is a sense in which nostalgia, and a belief in certain values which you wish to believe are still there, are very much part of what you write about.*

DP: I don't know 'nostalgia' ... I dislike nostalgia, you see. Nostalgia is a very second-order emotion. It's not a real emotion. What nostalgia does is what the realist in a sense does with what is in front of him; the nostalgiac looks at the past and keeps it there, which is what is dangerous about nostalgia, which is why it's a very English disease in a way – inevitable, given our decline, Imperial decline, if you like, so that there are sorts of cricks in the neck ... looking backward is part and parcel of our political language. But I'm not dealing in nostalgia. I don't believe that I'm dealing in nostalgia. I think that if you didn't have an alert awareness of the immediate past, then what you are actually doing is being complicit with the orthodoxy of the present, totally, and I am sometimes amused to be berated, to see myself berated as one who uses nostalgia, and this is not the case.

I've used the immediate past to intrude upon the present, so that it isn't a thing out there, the past, which is done with, it is actually running along beside us now, and its, its misconceptions and its values, and its correct conceptions can be seen just that degree more clearly, and using the forties and the war and the immediate post-war, or in *Pennies from Heaven* the mid-thirties was a way of, without being didactic or preachy or trying to draw political, social, you know, that sort of writing, just simply letting that time be in order to show what this time is like. So that's the opposite of nostalgia. Nostalgia says it's safety back there, and, Oh those dear dead days and all that, and wrings a tear from your eye, because they are unreclaimable, but I say they are reclaimable and that they are, that they are there and here.

AY: *What about, specifically with* Pennies from Heaven, *what were the aspirations of the Hoskins character in* Pennies from Heaven?

DP: The aspiration was about that oldest one, the songs that he was peddling were in a direct line of descent from the Psalms and they were saying no matter how cheap or banal or syrupy-syncopated they were, they were actually saying the world is other than it is. The world is better than this, and that what you, you the salesman, the Hoskins character, Arthur Parker, what you are feeling oppressed by or suffocated by, or what your yearnings are are these, and he believed in them, and that was his tragedy ... I mean, believing in such a simple belief is the same as believing in a very complex belief and can lead you to the same dilemmas, the same traps, if you like – the way that popular culture can in its very generality – and what distinguishes it, what separates it rather from considerable art is its generality – it doesn't ask anything specific or say anything specific, but what it does is draw out of you a specific.

There are people who look in birthday cards for the right verse, and it doesn't matter how cheap or that someone wrote twenty-four of them in the hour for his pay. What matters is the emotion that that verse is supposed to be hinting at, which in its generality allows the consumer, whether it's the popular song or the tabloid journalism or any one of those outlets of popular art so-called, to mingle in a way with its day and its time ... much more immediately sometimes than difficult art can do.

AY: *Was there a separation, would you say, in the thirties and forties between popular culture and the selling of ideas and products?*
DP: I think popular culture was more constrained, because there was another culture which was more dominant ... there were other sets of values going on at the same time, like the class thing, like the monarchy, you know, that whole ... I am using that as shorthand, obviously: there were other values which didn't appear to be in the market-place. Now, if you were talking about, for example, the monarchy, you would have to say that it

is an invention of the British Tourist Board. It appears to be that. It has become that; it hasn't become democratized, it has become commercialized. They are becoming more effective not in selling products but in selling the whole culture in which they are embodied, like little bits of fruit in a cake, the whole cake becomes a fruit cake. The whole television looks as though it's selling something, even the BBC.

Before that degree of commerciality, the public world was in the street and you could shut your door on it. And now it's here, it's in there (*points to head*), and as I'm not using it in a Marxist sense – I'm not trying to be tendentious but capitalism now is actually about selling all of you to all of you. But they don't know who it is they are selling. The only object is to keep in the game, which is to keep selling something, and one day we are going to find out what it is.

AY: *Well, if you have this cynicism really, which it is – or fear of what the mass media can do – how do you try to express true values, ideas with at least some conviction which won't be misunderstood because they are presented in the same form?*

DP: Principally by showing or by attempting to assert how sovereign you are as an individual human being, if you knew it. And that means contending with all the shapes, all the sort of half-shapes, all the memories, all the aspirations of your life – what, how they coalesce. How they contradict each other, how they have to be disentangled as a human act by you yourself. This sovereign self beyond, behind all those selves that are being sold things, remains the other unique, sovereign, individual.

AY: *Do you find that in order to find this self, this sovereign self, you have to retreat from the material world? I'm wondering if your illness . . . because you've used the analogy of retreat – a monastic analogy to describe life in a ward, a hospital ward?*

DP: That was only using the hospital in a sense of . . . in the proper use of the word retreat – that is, a withdrawal, not in order to disavow but in order to understand, in order to return to the world with better equipment. And it is undeniable that if you are in hospital for a long time, and you see it with the other patients, you see that odd, slightly menacing weird process beginning to grow in them where the outside world is seen as something else for the first time, and having to deal with the crisis of illness or whatever, and having most of them, say, having had to go to work every day, having to meet certain commitments all through life, no time to sit and think or lie and think, and that lying and thinking and dealing with crisis at the same means that you've been separated from the normal churning process of life into this monk-like semi-seclusion.

People say to me, you know, that must be autobiographical. I feel greatly offended when they do, because it's one of the least autobiographical pieces of work that I've ever attempted.

AY: The Singing Detective?

DP: Yes.

AY: *But you can't be surprised at people saying it's . . .*

DP: No, because I use, ultimately out of laziness, I would use the fact that the hero so-called – is it possible to have a hero, examine and discuss – the fact that he has arthritis and psoriasis, psoriatic arthropathy, and was, had a – I never at any stage in the script, incidentally, say the Forest of Dean – but that the child-hood area was the same as mine, and the disease was the same as mine, does not make it autobiographical. I could have given him some other interesting and cruel disease. Maybe I should have played around with a few diseases.

AY: *But you said somewhere that what's going on in your plays is what goes on inside people's heads, so to an extent isn't, aren't you going, aren't you drawing on that, even if you had to mask that sense of your own experience?*

DP: What I was trying to do with *The Singing Detective* was to make the whole thing a detective story, but a detective story about how you find out about yourself, so that you've got this superfluity of clues, which is what we all have, and very few solutions – maybe no solution – but the very act of garnering the clues and the very act of remembering, not merely an event but how that event has lodged in you and how that event has affected the way you see things, begins to assemble a system of values, and only when that system, no matter how tenuous it might be, is assembled was Marlow able to get up out of his bed, which is why it isn't about psoriasis or psoriatic arthropathy – or detectives, or that particular childhood, but about the way that we can protect that sovereignty that we have and this is all that we have and it is the most precious of all of the human capacities, even beyond language, even . . . it is the one – it's almost impossible to talk about it, because you're bumping against the very rim of communication when you try to talk about it, but by being able to use, say, the musical convention, and the detective-story convention and the 'autobiographical' in quotes convention, and making them coexist at the same time so that the past and the present weren't in strict sequence because they aren't – they are in one sense, obviously, in the calendar sense, but they're not in your head in that sequence and neither are they in terms of the way you discover things about yourself, where an event twenty years ago can become more – it can follow yesterday instead of precede it and that out of this morass, if you like, of evidence, the clues and searchings and strivings, which is the metaphor for the way we live, we can start to put up the structure called self . . . out of, out of which, out of that structure – we can walk out of that structure, saying at least I know and you know better than before what it is we are.

AY: *It is the illness, though, that is the catalyst which allows . . .*

DP: It is the . . . that is the crisis . . . it is the illness which has stripped him – it's the Job part, if you like, which is where the crisis . . . in dramatic terms, it needed exactly that, that starting point of extreme crisis and no belief, nothing except pain and a cry and a hate, out of which were assembled the fantasies, and the fantasies became facts and the facts were memories and the memories became fantasies and the fantasies became realities, and all of them became him and all of them allowed him to walk.

AY: *Now your work appears within the context that you've described – this rather dangerous context. How do you find that television ... you've said how you think television has changed, but do you feel it has changed beyond help and that the world as we, that we live in at the moment and that we are experiencing is one which is not moving in the right direction, or in a direction which is not exactly ...*

DP: I don't know what direction the world is moving in and in that sense I'm quietist in that I ... I do care, but I don't care in the way that I want to scream in the street about it. All I know is that if you ... you have to attend to that which you can attend to, and in my case obviously it's ... I do have a very ... I have, to use another – I mean, I've been spilling out antique words, but I have, I do feel that I have a sense of vocation and I didn't know that I had this and I've discovered it with gratitude and relief late in the day, but having got it and so that I can almost hold it, I'm not going to let it go. I'm therefore attending, or showing in that Quaker sense of the word concern means – it doesn't mean that you issue a diatribe of where you think society is going to or ... it doesn't mean that I'm feeling any the less passionately involved in what I think is wrong, but that if I do what I can do myself with the pen on the page, within the very medium that seems the most, seems to be the voice of the occupying power, then the resistance ought to take place within the barracks as well as outside.

'Last Pearls'

There came a day when Jack should have acknowledged that the writing had to stop. Perhaps it was the same day that the punctuation marks decided of their own will to mess about with their functions and their shapes. A comma that had been lying around ready for use started to wriggle at the edge of his vision like the worm it had so often threatened to be, and then tried to scoop up a subordinate clause he had had no intention of using.

'What is this? What is going on?' Jack asked out loud, although he was fairly sure there was for the moment no one else watching him in this odd-angled room at the top of the old house. But he could never be quite sure, so swiftly did the shapes come and go.

And now a slightly chipped full-stop would not cease rolling loose along the top of the line, even when it bumped into another of its kind. The collision meant there was not enough space to complete the exposition. *Chink!* The sentence had to shorten had to shor had to *shh*.

'No, no,' he muttered, asserting his strength and reason for another few seconds.

He knew full well that these words and their accompanying marks had no volition. They could not be independent of his control. The writer was sovereign. It had always been up to Jack to make of these letters what he willed. Long slopes, smooth glides, shining cusps, abrupt halts, his pen weaving and willowing across the empty landscape.

But Jack had been on morphine for fifteen weeks now, at a steadily increasing rate. Hobgoblin images wafted or sculpted by the opiates contended with the sharper, cannibal bites of pain. His daily intake was now enough to stop a stampeding mastodon in its screaming tracks. Instantly, the beast formed itself with a

75

savage undulation of trunk and threatening crash of feet, before spinning off into a grey whirl at the corner of the desk where something else cackled out of a wet mouth. Get off! Get away!

A syringe-pump hung about Jack's now emaciated torso, regularly and inexorably jerking the colourless poison into his veins. Diamorphine was his dearest friend, and his most threatening foe, clearing space up ahead where he could fight these words in pain-free passages – but then closing it down again under amorphous blankets of suffocating numbness or lurid solicitation.

His task was to complete, and to burnish with good, a story that he had scarcely started when the awful diagnoses had arrowed through the pain and the bewilderment. He saw three big billboard posters being pasted up at the crossroads just ahead. CANCER. INOPERABLE. THREE TO SIX MONTHS. Oh, God – would every thought, every emotion, now turn on its back and slither towards the one thought, death, and the one emotion, fear?

Jack found that it was not so. He was burning to right the wrongs he had inflicted on his own talent in the last piece of work he had had published, a tawdry narrative called *Black Pearls*. The pain he had already so stoically endured through a fatuous series of mis-diagnoses had left him with too great a residue of waste. He sensed the rapidly growing tumour smack in the middle of his body (his soul?) as something that stood for all the sloth, the bile and the ill-will of the world. In a sudden incandescent flare of what must be joy, he determined to counter these common malignancies with the grace of – his face twisted for a second into the sardonic – with the grace of Art.

Black Pearls had been about a writer who had completed his novel and then found, at first to his whimsical amusement, that many of the events and some of the dialogue in the story were repeating themselves in front of him, even as he walked along the street. There –! That black bin-liner bag blowing against the spiked rail. It had opened a paragraph on the last but one page of *Black Pearls*.

The coincidence of blown bag and spiked railing, shaped just thus, exactly on the beat of his old sentence, intrigued and challenged him, and he began to see many other such small juxtapositions as he settled with a lurch of pain at the continent of his desk. There were doorways back into the novel he had come to hate. The conviction was growing upon him that *Black Pearls* had somehow or other escaped into the world in the same way a virus might. How could it have been, he asked himself in a spurt of bitter agony, that in the wonder of good health and the serenity of his life as it had been, he had created a narrative that reeked with despair and evil, a negation of the human spirit?

The critics had loved it.

Jack now saw it as his moral duty to staunch the bilious leak between his last piece of fiction and the world out there in front of him. He could see now with all the clarity of a real sickness that the sour book he had published just six months before was not a worthy – no, not even a *safe* book to be wandering about the streets or slithering with reptilian glints into the various interstices of the day, someone else's day.

Now that he was so mortally ill, and all the barriers had crumpled, he could at last acknowledge how wicked it was to stain the sensibilities of his readers with arty filth. Genuinely nasty things had happened in that last novel: wanton cruelties and unnecessary little flicks of sadism made worse by being funny as well. And (he saw the bin-bag again) if any of these made-up events were by some necromancy coming true *out there*, then it was imperative that he divert them back onto other pages. He would cleanse them in the process. These would be the pages he was now writing, pristine at last. A tilt against the dragon.

Jack discovered that if he began to write at about half-past four in the morning, when a pale bruise of light edged nervously around the sides of the window, his mind was clear enough of the clogging dirt and his body sturdy enough to push away the rodentine pain for at least three and a half hours at a go, as freely as though the words had never been used before. He was turning black pearls into white ones.

Line by line, paragraph by paragraph, tugged free of morphine phantoms, Jack's resolve became an exultation as it fought across the pages. Much of the story came out in the dangerous present tense, for it was this which kept beckoning the most urgently at him. The pen bites into the smooth white, the thought pushes up on the crossbow of the way he carved his 't', and for minutes, no, hours at a time he was able to shove away the glowering imminence of his own demise in the everlasting glory of making words in the here, just *here*, and the now, just *now*.

Present tense called up first person. Jack makes his 'hero' walk with him in the arduous journey out of life. He revisits the places in the plot where the darkened thoughts of *Black Pearls* had found restless habitation. He is encountering once more the curdled beings who had in his new opinion sleazed and soiled the original story.

Each tough session is completed with a half-sigh, half-grunt of weary satisfaction: the sound of a wrong being put right. Then the diamorphine wheedles its way deeper, the eyelids cannot lift their own sudden weight, the face pinches in to defend itself against the mimicries of sleep as they insinuate through grotesqueries gnarled by the slightest change of position or the most miniscule shift of light. Objects float past, unanchored by consecutive thought.

And each night while he bubbled, murmured and sometimes cried out in the more fetid patches, two other pairs of eyes would briefly scan what had been written. His wife and his daughter looked at the words, looked at each other, sometimes smiled, sometimes cried, and said little. They approved of his daily combat, which meant the prolongation of his own sense of self-hood and self-purpose, thus tempering much of their own grief.

'I have to work. Have to. Do you understand? There are serious wrongs to put right. So many things to correct,' he would say to the first of the two fair, green-eyed heads that poked almost tentatively around his door in the early morning.

Bzz-zup went his self-driven syringe. A scatter of spiky adjectives knelt at the edge of the line before deciding that one of them was a Prussian helmet about to be purred at and stroked by a slinky cat.

'Of course we understand. Of course you must work. It's wonderful to see that you can!'

The desk opened up into a big hole, but he was able to close it with a half-turn of his own head. The grains decided to dance in the wood, but kept clear of the white page.

'*Black Pearls!*' he said once, in a hiss of venom which startled the mild-mannered GP. The visiting doctor had not read the novel, but he had heard it spoken of as one of the best of its kind for years. Spare, truthful, bleak, a story about the last things that never strayed into the morbidly sanctimonious. Hadn't it won some prize or something? One of the very literary, prestigious ones?

The black bin-liner bag had blown against the spiked rail again, so Jack knew that he had reached the final pages of his new and, he believed, his greatest work. Just in time! The pen itself insisted upon changing its slender configuration, becoming stumpy in the clenched hand. The full-stop continued to roll, alternately an irritating piece of grit and a smoothly shiny billiard ball. And then the desk itself bounced upwards in rebellion to smack him hard under the chin.

'Just one more paragraph!'

That was the last thing he said before the great swamp of opiates sucked him under. But the injunction was easy enough for someone to execute. Jack had rewritten *Black Pearls* word for word. Everyone agreed that as an act of memory alone it was a formidable achievement.

He must have loved that book heart and soul, they said.

Works by
Dennis Potter

PLAYS FOR TELEVISION

1965
The Confidence Course
Alice
Stand Up, Nigel Barton
Vote, Vote, Vote for Nigel Barton

1966
Emergency – Ward 9
Where the Buffalo Roam

1967
Message for Posterity

1968
The Bonegrinder
Shaggy Dog
A Beast with Two Backs

1969
Moonlight on the Highway
Son of Man

1970
Lay Down Your Arms
Angels Are So Few

1971
Paper Roses
Traitor
Casanova

1972
Follow the Yellow Brick Road

1973
Only Make Believe
A Tragedy of Two Ambitions

1974
Joe's Ark
Schmoedipus

1975
Late Call

1976
Double Dare
Brimstone and Treacle
(*transmitted 1987*)
Where Adam Stood

1978
The Mayor of Casterbridge
Pennies from Heaven

1979
Blue Remembered Hills

1980
Blade on the Feather
Rain on the Roof
Cream in My Coffee

1985
Tender is the Night

1986
The Singing Detective

1987
Visitors

1988
Christabel

1989
Blackeyes

1993
Lipstick on Your Collar

1994
(*to be produced*)
Karaoke
Cold Lazarus

FILMS

Pennies from Heaven (1981)
Brimstone and Treacle (1982)
Gorky Park (1983)
Dreamchild (1985)
Track 29 (1987)
Secret Friends (1992)
Midnight Movie (1993)
Mesmer (1994)
White Clouds
   (1994; *to be produced*)

STAGE PLAYS

Vote, Vote, Vote for Nigel Barton
(1968)
Son of Man (1969)
Only Make Believe (1974)
Brimstone and Treacle (1977)
Sufficient Carbohydrate (1984)

NOVELS

Hide and Seek (1973)
Pennies from Heaven (1981)
Ticket to Ride (1986)
Blackeyes (1987)

NON-FICTION

The Glittering Coffin (1960)
The Changing Forest: Life in the
Forest of Dean Today (1962)